The Fighting Spirit of Judo
THE TECHNIQUE AND SPIRIT TO WIN

Yasuhiro Yamashita

11th August 1984, 23rd Olympics in Los Angeles Open Category Final against Mohammed Rashwan (Egypt).

Published in 1993 by Ippon Books Ltd
Unit 4, Wyllotts Manor,
Potters Bar, Hertfordshire EN6 2HN

First published in Japanese in 1991
under the title Tokon no Judo by
Baseball Magazine, Tokyo, Japan

ISBN 1874572 15 1

Reprinted 1999

Acknowledgements
Ippon Books is grateful to Sarah Cousens who translated the major part of
Tokon no Judo and co-ordinated the remainder.
Thanks also go to David Finch for extra photographs, Duncan Steet for edit-
ing the English text, Edward Ferrie for laying it out, and Adam Green for
output and reprographics.

Printed in Great Britain by Redwood Books, Trowbridge, Wiltshire

Foreword

One of the many pleasures of life is to be emotionally moved by another person. Although it was almost seventeen years ago, I remember being moved when a young man with a boyish face caught my attention in my home town of Kumamoto. I knew instantly that this particular young man had world class potential.

Two years later, he was defeated in the semi-final of the National High School tournament. I was deeply moved by the way in which, despite his loss, he competed in a dignified and sportsman-like manner. That young man was Yasuhiro Yamashita. His achievements since then are already well-known.

The reason why Yamashita appeals to so many people is of course, because of his brilliant technique, but also, in my view, because his techniques express his personality. There are many people who can do traditional or brilliant techniques but those who manage to attain a feeling of oneness in their spirit and technique are rare. From an early age, Yamashita was such a player.

I expected great things of Yamashita and he more than lived up to my expectations. However, these were not confined by the red *tatami*. I wanted him to study his chosen skill ever more diligently and in addition, apply the main principles in everyday life.

' *When before us there is no road, we should make a road behind us.*'

I hoped that Yamashita would walk the path of a pioneer as embodied by the above saying. It is my great pleasure to say a few words on the occasion of this new technical publication and extend this hope to all his future endeavours.

March 1991

Matsumae Shigeyoshi
Tokai University President
International Judo Federation Chairman

The Fighting Spirit Of Yashuhiro Yamashita
Kanji brushed by the author

Introduction

I was very big when I was a child. I'd get into fights and make my opponents cry and on the way home from school, I'd discard my bag and run around the hills and fields. My misdemeanours and obesity naturally worried my mother, so she took me along to the local *dojo*. This was in the spring of my fourth year at primary school. In retrospect it was, for me, a fateful encounter.

Since then I have grown up with judo. What I am today has been shaped entirely by judo. I would like to thank my parents, all the *sensei* who have guided me in my career; Shiraishi *sensei* and Sato *sensei* and all my *sempai*. Especially I gratefully acknowledge the immense support given by Matsumae Shigeyoshi *sensei*, president of Tokai University. The realisation of my childhood dream, of seeing the Japanese "*Hi no Maru*" flag being raised at the Olympics was realised in Los Angeles through the support and encouragement of friends and colleagues.

It may be presumptuous of me, but I am basing this book of techniques on my own favourite techniques. Not that I didn't think twice about exposing my limited knowledge to the public but I am following the publisher's wishes in strictly confining the subject matter to consideration of my favourite techniques and my approach to contests. I can only indulge in the hope that my personal experience might perhaps be of some use to my *kohai*.

Nowadays, I spend every day teaching. From this standpoint I am only too aware that when it comes to contests, we in Japan face very tough international competition. Of course, winning isn't everything in judo as in any other sport but, for me, in contest, winning is indeed everything. This is because, if this is our ultimate aim, and we put all our strength into it, everything else will come to us.

With this in mind, I have not gone beyond my own techniques in this book, though it was my intention to recollect the spirit, techniques and physical training of the days when I was a player, and nothing would give me greater pleasure than if this were to be of some use to the coaches and players of today. Furthermore, as I am still practising myself, I would welcome any reader's comments on this book.

Also I would like to thank Mr. Ikuo Ikeda of Baseball Magazine for all his trouble on my behalf.

Yasuhiro Yamashita

Contents

Chapter 1.   How to achieve maximum power

Introduction...14; Reasons for sustained success...16; Basic principles ...18; Thinking for oneself...21; Turn your weaknesses into weapons...24; Learn from others –everyone has a chance ...27; Learn from your defeats - do not be afraid of failure...29 Positive thinking...32; How to relax...34; When the going gets tough...37; Assume the worst...40; Overcoming the pressure of expectations...42; Knowing your opponents...45; Don't count your chickens–the Moscow Olympic Games...47; Enthusiasm on the wane - the battle with apathy ...49; A desperate situation at the Los Angeles Olympics...51; My last All-Japan championship–judo does not belong to me alone...54:

Chapter 3 Katame-waza — 135

Contest Tips 6 How to finish it quickly — 143

How to Achieve Your Maximum
Power and Skill

Introduction

According to the record book I have participated in 559 competitions (in fact more than that number if grading and training competitions are included) over 14 years between the ages of thirteen and twenty-seven when I retired from active judo. Retrospective analysis shows that over the final 8 years of that period I had 203 successive wins. At the time I could not afford to break my concentration on judo in order to look back over my record, and was unaware of this series of wins. No matter how good people thought I was, I always felt I was not yet at the top. It was only when I was free from all the tensions as a competitive player that I became confident enough to think of the significance of my record.

In an individual sport such as judo, there is always one who is victorious and one who is defeated. Ambition and competitiveness are natural functions of human behaviour, but one forms one's character when overcoming one's egoism and arrogance. I tried very hard to achieve this objective in judo.

In competitions, one is either on the offensive or on the defensive. In either case, if you have a lack of confidence, the result of a fight will be a foregone conclusion. Even if you have evident disadvantages, you should not give up and if you are apparently much superior to your opponent, you should not be off your guard. I have always fought in the belief that the result of a contest was never decided until the end of the fight. No matter how strong you are, you cannot be sure you will always win.

This chapter is about the lesson I learned from my experiences in my judo career.

My home town is Kumamoto in Kyushu, the southern Japanese island, where the master swordsman, Miyamoto Musashi ended his eventful life. In 1645 he wrote '*Gorin no Sho*'(The Book of Five Rings) at the age of 62. At the beginning of the chapter of Earth he wrote,

"I fought sixty times with various strategists without defeat, between the age of thirteen and twenty-eight or twenty-nine. When I looked back over my past at thirty years of age, I found that I had not mastered the strategy of swordsmanship but that I had won because I had a natural talent and followed a natural law. I did not have sufficient knowledge of other strategies. I wanted to understand further the nature of things in depth and trained my-self from morning to evening everyday. I then finally found my strategy. That was when I reached fifty years of age. "

Even Miyamoto Musashi trained every day, for almost twenty years in search of perfection in swordsmanship, from the age of thirty onwards. When I think that his fights must have been for life or death, I have to recognise the depth and severity of the world of martial arts. On this point I am not sufficiently matured to talk about victory. All I can offer here is a record of a judo player's career.

Reasons for sustained success

My record of 528 wins, 16 defeats and 15 draws, which surprises me even today, can be put down to the following factors:

1.   I was never satisfied with my achievements, so I was striving for a better result all the time.
2.   I was determined to realise my childhood dream.
3.   I was fortunate enough to have the right associates and circumstances.
4.   I was very healthy and strong.

My ideal judo strategy was to find one's opponent's weakness, apply one's strong point to his weak point and defeat him by an incisive technique, i.e. take the enemy by surprise. Although this sounds easy, it is not easy to do . I regard only sixty to seventy per cent of my results as being satisfactory. Therefore, I never felt that I had really mastered an incisive technique.

Secondly, my childhood dream was to win a gold medal in the Olympic Games. I was very much impressed when watching the Tokyo Olympics on television. This was when I was in my first year at primary school. My ultimate target was a gold medal while my immediate target was to win each contest.

Thirdly, I was fortunate to have good instruction, training partners and facilities. I was able to come to Tokyo to devote myself to practising judo at Tokai University. Then, after graduating , I was privileged to be able to spend a great deal of time practising judo while I was working as a teacher. My record could not have been as it is without such support and understanding and I will always be very grateful for it.

Lastly, I inherited health and strength from my parents and my grandfather. I broke my left ankle just after the Japanese government decided not to send participants to the Moscow Olympics, I remember my doctor was astonished by how strong my bones were.

Basic principles

I had three judo teachers, Mr. Seiki Fujitsubo and Mr. Reisuke Shiraishi in Kumamoto and Mr. Nobuyuki Sato in Tokyo. I owe a great deal to them for my success.

I was taken to Mr Fujitsubo's dojo at the age of 9. My parents hoped that I would lose weight if I learnt judo, since I was too fat and that it would knock me into shape in other ways as well. They were delighted with the result although I didn't lose any weight.

I started judo seriously when I was head hunted from my primary school by Mr Shiraishi who was the judo supervisor at Toen Junior High School in Kumamoto. In order to attend my new school, I had to go and live with my grandfather in Kumamoto. I was very much influenced by my grandfather. He always accompanied me to competitions whether in Japan or abroad. At home he cooked our meals himself and he came to school to watch me practice almost every day.

Judo practice at Junior High School was very demanding. I got so tired that I often went to sleep on the bus and missed my stop. However, under Mr Shiraishi's tutelage I managed to change from right- to left-handed and I became a medium weight player .

At the age of 12 I was 172 cm high and weighed 78 kg and by the time I was 15 my height had increased to 180cm and I weighed 120 kg. Mr Shiraishi told me: "In the future when you fight in Japanese or world championships, your opponents will be heavier than you are." Therefore, I was not allowed to use techniques such as *maki-komi* which take advantage of heavy weight. In order to develop a quicker style of judo, he laid down the following guidelines:

1. Techniques must be done on the move
2. Work on *ashiwaza*
3. Avoid taking a deep grip.
4 Never use *maki-komi*
5. Develop combinations of three or four techniques.

These became the basis of my judo. Mr Shiraishi gave the judo club members the following moral guidance:

1.   The objective of judo is to become a good citizen so you must persevere with your studies as well as judo. If you try, you can do it.
2.   According to the proverb; "The boughs that bear most hang lowest." Be modest, obedient and polite in order to become strong.

3.   "A tiger leaves his skin at his death. In the same way, one should leave one's name after one's death." Everybody has the potential to reach the top. I wish to have one or two famous judo players from this club.

This moral guidance certainly encouraged a change in my personality for the better. Mr Shiraishi had a difficult time training us as I, for one, had been a naughty boy before I started judo.

One day he brought a television set to the dojo to show a national team contest. He said, "These players are the ones you will compete with in the future." It hardly seemed realistic to regard ourselves as members of the national team. We did not know his intention at that time, whether he was testing our enthusiasm or just encouraging us. Whatever his motive, I believed what he said.

I was given two targets: to be the high school champion at fifteen and to be the Japanese champion at eighteen.

Thinking for oneself

As well as winning the junior high school national championship, I did indeed become the high school champion. However the following year I was defeated in the semi-final by Isao Matsui. I was devastated by this defeat and, realising it was time for a change, my grandfather urged me to go to Tokyo in order to be at the centre of things. So, I moved to Tokai University High School where I was made very welcome. I must express my indebtedness to both Mr Shiraishi and Mr Sato for their affection and the education they gave me.

While I was studying at Tokai University Sagami High School, I practised judo with the members of Tokai University

Judo Club. I was very fortunate to have such good practice facilities during this period. Mr Sato who was the manager of the club at Tokai gave me three tips which improved my skill.

1. Do not pride yourself on your judo. There have been few judo players of real genius. The trouble is that the stronger you become, the more attention you will receive. If you start getting spoiled, you will lose. You are not top of the world rankings yet.

2. Try not to get injured. No matter how strong you are, you cannot fight if you are injured or ill. The fact is that injury and illness are mostly preventable. You have to practise within your limits. Gradually you will be able to extend those limits but on the other hand, you must take care of yourself as you may become too tired mentally and physically. You have to be brave enough to refuse invitations and distractions.

3. You have to realise that you have only one chance at each level of a tournament. But, if you seize that opportunity, you will get another.

I was already widely tipped as one of the most promising judo players of the period and Mr Sato felt I might be contented with my present standard if he did not warn me against becoming big-headed. At seventeen it was timely advice, as was the advice that you have only one chance. This insight was based on his personal experience. He missed his chance of winning at the Olympics as judo was not included in the Mexico Olympics when he was at his peak. At the next Olympics in Munich, he was injured during training with the USSR teams and as a result he did not get through the first round even though he should have been one of the major contenders. I was very moved by his experience. The reason I won so many contests in succession is because I never forgot his advice.

When I went to university, I lived with Mr Sato's family, and the evenings after dinner became very precious. While we enjoyed tea prepared by his wife, we discussed sportsmanship, education and life in general. I learned a lot from these discussions. He never imposed his will on me but merely gave me his advice. He liked me to take my own initiative.

When I narrowly beat Saito for my ninth title at the All Japan Championship, he said, "The reason I did not give you any advice is because my ideal player is not one who follows my advice, but one who thinks and acts for himself." When I think of his method of coaching, I can understand his philosophy. Nowadays a lot of new coaching methods are highly developed but after all, a win is achieved by oneself, not by the coach. In this way, I learned judo philosophy from our discussions after dinner.

Turn your weaknesses into weapons

I had a lot of disadvantages when I came to Tokyo. One of them was that I was physically weak. I hadn't done enough physical training. I was not good at *newaza* and thirdly, I could not cope with a competitor who took an opposite (*kenka-yotsu*) grip and reached over from above. I was regarded as a genius, but to an expert's eye I was immature. I made special efforts to overcome these three weaknesses. Eventually they became my weapons.

I started training to develop muscle power. Running was not my favourite activity but when we had to go running I tried very hard not to lose sight of everybody. After my power increased through training, I was not defeated by that many strong foreign judo players. Even if you have only thirty to forty percent of the strength of your opponent, you may still have an advantage with superior technique. Technique defeats power.

Senior members of the club with whom I had the advantage in randori always teased me about my groundwork which was my greatest weakness. Honestly, I hated it. But one day, by chance, I defeated Sato *sensei* in groundwork. This proved to be a turning point in my performance. I recall this fight lasted about 20 minutes. I usually struggled against Sato *sensei*, but this time as if in a dream, I controlled him with *okuri-eri-jime* while putting the strangle on – a technique often used by Sato *sensei* himself. I came round on top of him with my weight and the contest was over. I couldn't believe it! Later lying in bed and thinking of this lucky win, I suddenly became confident that I would no longer be defeated by the senior club members, as I had defeated Sato *sensei*, an expert at groundwork. Gradually I became so confident that I came to believe that nobody could defeat me at groundwork. Moreover as soon as opponents went into groundwork, I was confident in the result of the fight. Of course senior club members stopped teasing me about my groundwork after that.

Age does not automatically give you superiority in competitive judo. Senior members are often afraid of being defeated by younger players so they make sarcastic remarks. In such cases you should not be timid as the result of this abuse of seniority, on or off the mat .

By practising with my university colleagues, I overcame my third weakness which was a vulnerability to the opponent catching the back of my collar over my shoulder. If I could, I avoided this grip. If I could not avoid it, I attacked the opponent with *kosoto-gari*. At once my weakness became a strong point. Most people never realised that this grip was once my weakness. Everybody has his weakness. If you want to win, it is very important to conquer your weakness. There is always a way to turn it to your advantage.

Learn from others – everyone has a chance

Physical strength is an important factor in becoming a strong judo player. However, no matter what your physique, the following advantages should be available to all :

1. Good advice from teachers.
2. Time to work out your strategy by yourself.
3. Picking up useful information at every opportunity.

It is very important that you have the determination to be a better player, and you believe in yourself. If you try, you can do it. Do not waste any opportunity to learn something. Twenty-four hours a day are given to everybody equally. Progress depends on how you use your time. I always try to watch other people practising in order to learn from them. Don't waste your time while waiting for your turn. Rather, you should take the chance to observe. Moreover, when you cannot practise due to an injury, you should concentrate on watching other people practise. When you are watching other people, you should focus on their techniques which you want to overcome. By watching, I learned to overcome my aversion to a deep collar grip. While I was training at the All Japan team camp in my second year at high school, I learned how to improve my *osoto-gari*, counters, body control, groundwork etc. from the senior members. At this training camp I was able to pick out my future rivals' techniques and skills. In the same way, I felt that everybody was taking note of whatever I did. Especially when I felt my rival, Saito, watching me, I moved out of his sight in order not to let him become familiar with my techniques. On the other hand when I practised with lesser players, I let them use their favourite technique and I gauged the potential of the technique. By understanding its effectiveness, one could avoid any nasty scares. I made good use of this training method against players who might possibly become my rivals in the future.

Even off the mat there are opportunities to gain useful information; whatever you are doing be it watching television, reading newspapers, or having a chat with your friends at the pub you should not lose any opportunity.

Sometimes at practice or in competitions you are unexpectedly successful with a good technique. Do not think you were just lucky. You should analyse the situation and try it again. You should develop your 'accidental' success into a greater repertoire. Always ask questions and do not rest until you have the answer. At school I asked questions all the time.

Learn from your defeats – do not be afraid of failure

My 16 defeats occurred over four years between the ages of sixteen and nineteen. I was defeated most often during the period between the ages of seventeen and eighteen. During these four years, I had achieved my goal of entering the All-Japan competition and dreamed of representing Japan. At that time in the heavy-weight category, Haruki Uemura (Asahi Kasei), Sumio Endo (Metropolitan Police), Kazuhiro Ninomiya (Fukuoka Police) and Chonosuke Takagi (Keishicho) were all in fierce competition with each other. In order to gain the All-Japan title and to represent Japan, I had to defeat all of them. As they were very strong, I was often defeated within an inch of winning.

The record of my hard-fought games over one year from 1975 shows how difficult it was to win against those strong players. Over that period I was defeated twelve times, four defeats by Uemura, four by Endo, two by Ninomiya, and one each by Anzai and Takagi. If I took a step forward, I was knocked down, and if I tried something else, I was knocked down again. However, at every contest I improved, as I was at the age when one makes rapid progress.

I sometimes cried in frustration when I felt I had really let myself down. But, it is important that you do not hesitate to analyse how you have been defeated and that you put your experience to practical use. In this way, good can come out of failure.

One particularly bad experience of mine (I might even say disgraceful) was in the final at the All-Japan Students Competition in 1977. Having won the Japanese champions' title before this competition, I was winning without a hitch at this tournament. Then, in the final I faced Tsuyoshi Yoshioka (from Chuo University) whom I had first defeated in our high school days. While everything is going well, one can sometimes meet with an unexpected failure if one relaxes. I never imagined I would lose against Yoshioka whom I had defeated only the year before. As soon as the fight ended, I thought I had won by a small margin, but in fact, Yoshioka won by a split decision. It was hard to describe my disappointment since I felt that I was winning during the fight. Mr Sato reprimanded me: "Make no judgement about winning or losing, and concentrate on applying your strength and techniques. Your attitude towards the fight decided the result." I had failed to make the best of myself. I was probably too big-headed thinking that since I was number one in Japan I would not lose. I was ashamed that I had not realised that I was number one only by a thin margin.

From this time on I resolved to concentrate on achieving my maximum ability and on fighting in such a manner that no one could possibly question the result.

One can never predict the result of a fight with certainty. Anything can happen. I never forgot this bitter experience and this defeat was my last.

Positive thinking

One naturally becomes edgy before a
fight and I used to find that if a trivial
matter weighed on my mind, it always disturbed my sleep. Anxiety causes loss of
judgement and in judo as in everyday life
you should always maintain your mental
equilibrium; easier said than done. Every
event or word can be interpreted in a different way depending on one's character. I am
a very optimistic person, and this has been
an advantage in my career.

When I was selected for the Tournoi de
Paris in 1976, my Japanese rivals told me
before my departure to Paris that European judo players are very big, with arms
like tree trunks and with chest hair like
brillo pads. I swallowed the whole story but
when I got there, I discovered to my relief
that they were no bigger than I was, and my
confidence was restored. Incidentally in
the semi-final Wallace of Australia countered my first attempt at *osoto-gari* by using
ashibarai and got a *waza-ari* (*ippon* by the
referee). I soon recovered with my groundwork. Foreign players were tough, but not
invincible.

At the 10th world championship in Spain in 1977 it was predicted that I would come up against Sergei Novikov (USSR) who had won a gold medal in the Montreal Olympics. I was not at all confident that I would defeat him so I convinced myself that it would not be my fault if I lost since he was the best in the world and I would blame the Japanese Judo Association for sending a mere 20 year old to this championship. In this way I could feel more optimistic about the competition. However, it never took place due to a political problem and then when it was cancelled, I had to try hard to make myself believe that it did not matter that there was no chance to compete.

The world championship, as well as the All-Japan and the Olympics, is one of the biggest events judo players dream of competing in. I had won a place at the championship after a fierce battle with my old rival, Endo. It seemed intolerable not to be able to fight after all the intense training we had put in for this competition. Then later, I had to go through the same experience once again with the Moscow Olympics.

When I first heard the news, I confined myself to my room because I did not want to see anyone or to hear any sympathetic remarks. Usually I can change my mood easily but this time it took me a long time to get over my disappointment. However, a few days later, I went to the pub near my training digs with my best friend and managed to drown my sorrows.

How to relax

Pre-contest nerves are a constant problem for competitors as, in order to fight to your true ability you should be relaxed. I know what it is like to be too stressed to perform to your best ability at a crucial moment. I would be very surprised if there is anyone in the world who does not get cold feet sometimes. The fact is that everybody feels nervous before a big event. The important thing is to overcome one's nervousness.

In my case I would get nervous in the two weeks before competitions such as the All-Japan championships. During that period I would become tense and depressed. However there are ways to get over this sort of problem.

For example:

1. I would pick up waste paper to clean up the road. If I bump into a beautiful lady or it is a fine day I would interpret these things as good omens.

2. I listen to classical music in which I am not normally interested.

3. If I find myself yawning before a contest, I take a deep breath to refresh my body.

4. When you are nervous, you always feel like going to the toilet. Do not resist this feeling it. By going to the toilet you can get the poisons out of your system.

1. The first time I ever competed in the world championship was in Paris in October 1979. The senior members of the Japanese team tended to stay in their rooms and read books but I thought that staying in a small room for a long time would be too stressful. So I went for a walk with Kiyoto Katsuki who was a fellow

Japanese competitor in the 71kg category. By singing popular songs, sitting on a bench watching passers-by and taking a deep breath occasionally I soon felt refreshed and thanks to this light recreation, I ate and slept well.

I learned how important relaxation is when you are tuning up before a big competition. At home I often climbed up to the top of the small hill called Mt. Kobo. I felt I could gain vital energy by taking in the fresh air and listening to birds singing.

2. In the Los Angeles Olympics in August 1984 I was given special permission to have one day off which I spent in the Japanese quarter having a Japanese meal and going shopping. When I returned to the Olympic village, I went round a few times in the bus. Then in order to get enough exercise, I took a sauna and swam in the pool. Thanks to my enjoyable day I was able to relax over the evening meal and slept well at night. This one day dispelled the heavy atmosphere of stress in the village.

These are my methods of relaxation for reduction of tension and nerves.

When the going gets tough........

    It is not always possible to ensure that every event goes as smoothly as the Paris championships. At the USSR International Judo Competition held in Tblissi in the Georgia Republic in February 1978 there was one problem after another. It was a long journey from Japan to the middle of Asia. In addition, the people of Tblissi are renowned for their love of martial arts, and the crowd and judges were rather partisan. Then there was a mistake in the transportation and the judogi for the Japanese team did not arrive at the hotel. To cap it all, my main opponent would be the USSR hero Sergei Novikov who had won a gold medal at the Montreal Olympics and I had to face him in the second round of the qualifying competition. I had never experienced such a combination of jet-lag, lack of tuning, unfavourable venue, and unlucky draw. However, there was no use being pathetic when confronting Novikov with an enthusiastic crowd behind him. The only thing I could do was to take a defiant attitude.

I told myself before the fight, "I will do my best. If I lose, I'll put it down to the poor conditions." The result was that I defeated Novikov by a small margin in the qualifying match and again in the final. I gained a lot of confidence by winning in spite of everything.

In November of the same year, the first Jigoro Kano International Judo Competition was held in Japan for the centenary anniversary of the Kodokan. I faced a field which included Novikov, Jean-Luc Rougé (France), Dietmar Lorenz (East Germany) in both the 95kg and open-weight categories. I will never forget this competition.

I had a good start to the year winning in the International Competition in Tblissi but I had become mentally and physically tired after continuously competing: in Europe for three weeks followed by the All-Japan Student competition, the National Athletic Meet in Nagano, the world student championship and the All-Japan Select Competition. I was expected to win in two classes in the Kano cup and although I wanted to win, I was in a deep slump. Being distressed, I took Sato *sensei* into my confidence and asked to be excused from the official functions. He understood my position and made my excuses for me, although he was criticised for taking my side. I just managed to tune up before the competition with a sauna bath and massage and I achieved my objective. I defeated Uemura in the over 95kg class and Rougé in the open.

From my experience in the USSR Open and the Kano Cup I learned that concentration and effort is more important than physical condition. I believe that a desperate player can achieve at least 70 to 80% of his or her capability. The deeper the depression, the more one has to brace one's nerve and concentrate one's mind on the fight.

I always emphasise the importance of mental strength in my own judo. It is not an exaggeration to say that it was developed by my experiences at the above-mentioned two competitions. Later, in the Los Angeles Olympics I tore my calf muscle fighting Arthur Schnabel, but overcame the physical aspect of the accident and went on to win the following two fights and take the gold medal. I had to tell myself, "Do not show any pain. Fix your eyes on your opponent."

Assume the worst

One should always assume the worst case. Curiously enough everyone tends to indulge in wishful thinking. For example, Japanese players often assume the following conditions before they leave.

1. Japanese tatami mats will be laid.
   (Japanese tatami mats are very rare. Usually the mats are too soft.)

2. You can have Japanese meals.
   (Not usually.)

3. Referees will be fair.
   (If you think so, you will be very disappointed.)

4. Spectators will appreciate good judo no matter where the player comes from.
   (It is common knowledge that they support home players.)

5. Your greatest rival will not be in the same qualifying group.
   (Sometime you face him in the first round.)

If you make these sorts of assumptions, you may end up losing your cool and panicking. Unless competitions are held in your own country, you will face disadvantages.

Therefore I always assumed the worst case, and I tried to find a way to bring out my best under the circumstances. Of course, it is not always as bad as this. If circumstances turn out better than you expected, your morale will receive a boost and you may fight better because of it. Japanese players are often criticised for not performing to the best of their ability against foreign players. My view is that these disappointing results can be put down to the above mentioned items. If you wish to win abroad, it is important to assume every one of these disadvantageous circumstances. You have every reason to believe that you cannot fight abroad under the same conditions as at home, not only in judo but in every sport.

Overcoming the pressure of expectations

Everybody becomes tense during a fight irrespective of the scale of the competition. It was often said to me, "Losing doesn't occur to you does it? You enjoy your fight." It is not true. No matter how minor the fight is, tension builds up beforehand. When you are nervous your opponent's strong points appear much more significant. Then you get even more nervous. However, you do not have a chance if you are not tense before a fight as you cannot do your best without adrenaline. I told myself that it was natural and indeed necessary to be nervous before fights.

However, when you represent your school or your country, healthy nervous tension develops into pressure which can disturb your peace of mind. I was under heavy pressure at the 11th world championship in Paris in December 1979. It was the same as the tension I felt at the national competitions. The honour of Japan weighed heavily on me. I was worried about what people would think. I would not have been pressured if the headline was going to be "Yamashita lost.", but a report entitled "Defeat for Japanese Judo" had much more significance in my mind. Of course there was no other way than to do my best but I had to win a war of nerves before the competition began.

In order to overcome pressure the causes should be eliminated. It is important to make a study of your potential opponents before the fight, and also to assume that you will be fighting under the worst conditions as I mentioned above. Assuming that you have made every effort in your training, it is then a matter of concentration. If you do all this, there should be no cause for worry on the day.

In the world championship in Maastricht, the Netherlands, two years after the Paris world championship, I was twenty-four, the age at which players are generally at their peak. I was entered in two classes, the over 95 kg and the open. No Japanese judo player had ever entered two classes before so a great responsibility was placed on me. Though I say it myself my condition was perfect. In fact, in the over 95 kg class I won all five fights by ippon taking only 9 minutes 4 seconds overall to do it. I fought as I wished. However when I weighed myself the next morning, I had lost five kilos. I could not believe it. It could not have been the physical stress as at no time was I in trouble on the mat. It must have been the mental pressure. I had two days rest before the open which was held on the last day of the event. Although I had done well on the first day, I knew that I could not afford to relax and had difficulty in controlling my nerves.

Well, I won all four fights up to the final by ippon. Before the final in which I faced the European champion Reszko of Poland, I went over the fight in my imagination. I could only see one outcome. I could not imagine that he had any advantage over me at all. I had never felt so confident. The odd thing was that finding no faults in my judo made me feel uneasy, as I was aware that it could have lead to carelessness. I told myself, "He is the European champion, and this fight is the final of the world championship. Aren't you being over-optimistic?" All in all though, I was expecting to win with my groundwork, and in fact I won with my favourite strangle (*okuri-eri-jme*).

I learned a lot about overcoming pressure and anxiety caused by being expected to win from my experiences at this competition. I managed to overcame the pressure by believing in myself and by doing everything I could in training. When it came to the contest I did not allow myself to become weak and defensive. Everybody is nervous and anxious before a competition but from that time I have been able to mentally overcome my nerves

You could say that the international competitions which most influenced my development as a player were the USSR International Competition, the Kano Cup, and the world championship in Maastricht.

Knowing your opponents

Sun Tzu the great Chinese strategist said, "If one knows one's opponent and understands oneself, one never loses in a hundred battles." This is the invariable principle of strategy from the old days. However it is almost impossible to carry out this philosophy. Sun Tzu goes on, "If one knows oneself without understanding one's opponent, one sometimes wins and sometimes loses. If one has no knowledge of one's opponent and does not know oneself, there is uncertainty in the result of every battle." I agree with him.

I believe that I analyse my opponents more than any other player does. I used to play video tapes over and over again in order to memorise my opponents' techniques, movements and habits. In order to build up the analysis, I would listen to everybody's opinion. Before the fight I imagined how the fight would be conducted, and took every precaution against being defeated.

Some people despised me saying, "Yamashita is surprisingly small-minded." But I did not care what other people thought of my preparations. My belief was that I could fight best when I knew both about the opponent and my own condition.

Now I am a teacher, I explain to students the importance of analysing their opponents. Unfortunately, many of them make the mistake of thinking that as a result of analysis, they will come to the conclusion that their opponents are much stronger than they are and hence that there is no way to win. But they are putting the cart before the horse. However powerful the opponents are, you should analyse them to find the small chinks in their armour. Sometimes you may be better off not knowing the strength of your opponent, but in this case you will not be able to improve your defence.

Don't count your chickens: the Moscow Olympic Games

Sometimes things do not go as planned. This was the simple lesson learned from the Moscow Olympics. As I mentioned before it was my childhood dream to get a gold medal in the Olympics. My training as well as my life had been aimed at winning a gold medal. I even counted two chickens and indulged in the rather wishful thinking that I would win two gold medals, one each in Moscow and Los Angeles and that I would leave an indelible footprint on judo history. When I think about it, I was outrageously ambitious.

My plans came apart because Japan decided to boycott the Moscow Olympics. I heard the news when I was in Fukuoka to participate in the All-Japan Select competition the purpose of which was to make the final selection for the Olympics. The political decision not to take part in Moscow was academic for me as I broke the bone just above my left ankle in a qualifying contest against Endo. I attempted to counter Endo's strong attack by *kanibasami* and put myself out of commission. On that day it was brought home to me that everything did not always go my way and I had to start from the beginning again.

I still do not understand why Japan boycotted the Moscow Olympics. Not only myself but other potential participants must have felt the same way. It surprises me that the government does not take account of the feelings of athletes especially as in the case of the Olympics, many have only one chance to compete.

The American government boycotted the games in the USSR because of its military interference in Afghanistan, and the Japanese government followed suit. However, I was told that in the USA President Carter invited all the athletes to the White House to explain the circumstances and listened to the athletes' points of view. In Japan by contrast, I received only a written notification from the government. The Japanese Olympic Committee sent no word at all to the athletes. I understand the complexity of politics and diplomacy, but I must say that on the whole, Japan gives little encouragement to sports. I sincerely hope that such a boycott will not happen again.

The future is always uncertain. There is no future for those who do not value everyday practice as well as competition. It proved my mental immaturity that I lost my temper at the boycotting of the Moscow Olympics. As I was taught by Sato *sensei*, it is not appropriate in this world to take things for granted. I told myself that I should take no account of anything else but fighting to my best ability under all circumstances. This became my main objective.

In order to encourage me, many people said, "There is always the next Olympics in Los Angeles", but I did not want to think that far ahead. Moreover I resented their assumptions. In the world of judo one cannot be sure that the same person will be winning in four years time. As it happened I did represent Japan at the Los Angeles Olympics but I was the only one from the previous Olympic team.

Enthusiasm on the wane - the battle with apathy

After my victories in the two categories at Maastricht, I felt all my enthusiasm ebb away, and I did not know why. Nothing had changed, my life was centred around judo and I did my best in training. However, I had lost the desire to win.

At the All-Japan championship in 1982 I still managed to win despite my lack of enthusiasm. The more I thought about it, the more apathetic I became. My position as number one was being challenged by Hitoshi Saito (Kokushikan University) who had made rapid progress. Sato *sensei* gave me some bitter advice, "You have got too big for your boots. As a result you cannot get ippon from Saito, can you? It is immature to be so satisfied with yourself!"

It is very important to have rivals. I became combative once again because of the feeling that Saito was catching up on me. Judo requires harmony of mental stability, technique and physical strength. But when you have reached your peak physically and technically, your mental stability is the vital factor. It is the destiny of a human being that his physical strength declines as he grows older and around 1983 I began to feel a gradual waning of my physical power. That year I had a torn muscle in my right ankle in February 1983, and also a torn muscle in my left shoulder at the 13th world championships in Moscow in October.

As Judo is a very physical sport, it is no exaggeration to say that physical training decides the result of a fight when you have reached the point where you can no longer improve your physical power. You need regular training and it should be adapted to your training to your daily life, but what you should not do is to become exhausted. Do not forget that you need to sleep well and have a well-balanced diet. Even if you look after yourself, you cannot help declining physically. You have to make up for your decline of power not by over-training but by your high spirits. In my latter period as a player, I had to struggle relentlessly to gain power and spirit.

A desperate situation at the Los Angeles Olympics

I have already mentioned the pressure of nerves before a fight. As the day of my fight approached, I became more and more edgy. When I saw Hidetoshi Nakanishi (in the under 71kg class), fall to an injury, I felt even worse as he was younger than me. At the Olympics I was under heavier pressure than in any other previous competition.

Two images of myself came across my mind when I was alone: One had me waving to a large crowd of spectators with a gold medal, and the other had me hiding in the changing room after being defeated. These two images appeared and disappeared one after another in my mind. I had never had such an experience in my long career. I talked to myself in the mirror, "Be nervous; you mustn't be ashamed of being nervous. Be strong in your will to fight." Strangely enough I did not have any feeling of fighting for the sake of my country. I wanted to win for myself, not for my country.

Despite warming up carefully before the fight, I met with an unexpected disaster in the second round against Artur Schnabel of West Germany. I turned in for *uchimata* but felt a sudden pain in my pivoting foot. I walked as normally as possible in order not to let Schnabel know of the injury. However it must have been obvious because there was a general stir among the spectators. There was a torn muscle in my right ankle.

In the semi-final I was thrown by Laurent del Colombo of France. My injured right leg could not react quickly enough to avoid his right osoto-gari. I struggled to avoid conceding ippon but gave him the lead. However, I was determined that I should not come to the Olympics and lose through injury and counter-attacked as best I could. I managed to throw him with ouchi-gari and then held him down with yoko-shiho-gatame. How did I turn the fight around? Probably through my belief that I should do everything humanly possible to win.

The final brought me up against Mo-hammed Rashwan of Egypt. Sato *sensei* told me in the changing room that he wished to break off our master and pupil relationship after the final. He had every confidence in the outcome of the fight to come, which was a big encouragement for me. I was resolved to demonstrate every-thing Sato *sensei* had taught me and went to the competition arena with fresh deter-mination.

While I was waiting on a mat-side seat with my eyes closed, I could feel Rashwan come in. "Good heavens!" As soon as I opened my eyes, my eyes met his eyes, and I smiled unconsciously. Of course I could not smile in the back of my mind. And then Rashwan returned the smile. "Good. I will win!", I thought. His smile eased his antipathy towards me. The spectators must have thought I won easily, but I had to use all my strength to win, which I did with *osae-komi* (*Yoko-shiho-gatame*). My childhood dream had come true.

My last All-Japan championship – judo does not belong to me alone

I have never suffered as much as I did when training for my final All-Japan championship. Although I had recovered from the injury sustained in Los Angeles, I was mentally very low because my grandfather had died the year before, on the very day I was presented with a national honour. I tried everything I could to lift my spirit but in vain. I usually took a trip to Kansai for training, but I abandoned this due to my being off form. At the university dojo I was beaten by the students. They were worried and obviously thinking what is the trouble with Yamashita, he may lose this year's championship. I could not help giving that impression.

Neither my pride nor the encouragement from those around me gave any inspiration. I forced myself to train with a hundred students to lift my spirits and it suddenly struck me that having spent more than ten years practising with students, I never until then realised the importance of these practices and the support they gave me. My depression was lifted by realising how much help those people had given me.

At the beginning of this chapter I mentioned that in judo there was only one winner and one loser. In that sense the result of the fight depends on the individual player. However if one always regards a win as a purely personal victory, one fails to realise just how much support is given by other people.

I began to understand that I was a teacher of judo. Even if I lost in the first round, I promised myself I would teach my students that the most important thing in judo was to fight to the end to the best of your ability. Up to then I had been pursuing gold medals to the exclusion of all else, but I finally emerged from my self-absorption. I could say that I learned from my students as well as teaching them. Having fought bravely to reach the semi-final, one of my students Nagoyo Ogawa came face to face with me in the semi-final. It was very unusual for a teacher and student to meet in a major competition.

In the final I faced Hitoshi Saito. Saito was showing his fighting spirit but it did not bother me. For me it was more important that I should dominate the contest. During the fight I lost a point by falling while attempting a sasae-tsuri-komi-ashi. In order not to be defeated I had to continually attack with my favourite techniques. I believed my continuous attack would lead to a result but I was aware that throwing Saito was very difficult, if not impossible. When he became defensive, he was given a passivity warning which levelled the scores. The fight ended after ten minutes without a conclusive technique by either player and I was given the decision.

Thinking back, the result was as close as that of my first victory over Endo. There are those who think I that Saito and Endo both won their respective contests. The decision of the judges in a fight is very delicate. A proverb says, "Do one's best and leave the rest to Heaven." In the end you win as a result of doing your best. I regret that I didn't have a decisive win over Saito. However, I was not unhappy with my performance as I was recovering from a long depression.

This was to be the last fight of my career. This chapter ends with the mental attitude I have developed over my sixteen year career in judo.

Your opponent is not weak as you think.
Your opponent is not strong as you think.

An analysis of my favourite techniques

My favourite throwing techniques are *osoto-gari*, *ouchi-gari* and *uchi-mata*; on the ground my favourites are *kuzure-kami-shiho-gatame*, *yoko-shiho-gatame* and *okuri-eri-jime*. Some people say, "Yamashita's techniques are simple and not particularly remarkable." And other people say, "You cannot tell which technique Yamashita is going to use, *osoto-gari*, *ouchi-gari* or *uchi-mata*. Both remarks are correct.

I regard techniques which unbalance your opponent as important in judo, and combine two or three of these while moving. The combination of techniques will depend on the circumstances. In any case judgement must be instantaneous. There is not a moment to lose if your whole body is to react to your opponent's movement.

I was very wary of using techniques which make use of a deep over-grip by which you pull your opponent in towards you. I tried to use techniques which could be applied to any size player, larger or smaller.

I have summarised my fight strategy below:

1. surprise the opponent with unexpected techniques.
2. use techniques in a decisive manner to their conclusion.
3. use effective combinations.

My favourite throw is *osoto-gari*, this being my decisive technique. As for groundwork, I devoted myself to combining it

COMBINATION 1 — THROWING TECHNIQUES

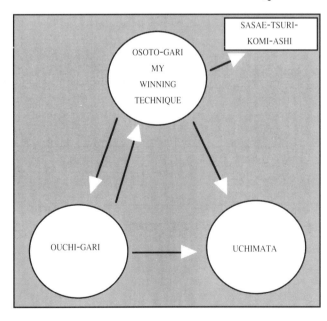

58

with throwing techniques and attacking from on top to use my weight efficiently. It did not suit me to take a sitting position or fight on my back. Large, round players like me are usually not good at groundwork from underneath. You can see my point if you look at a turtle lying on its back. Apart from ordinary practice sessions, you should not use techniques which you are not good at in competition. In fact I rarely found myself underneath my opponent in competition, so although I practised a lot, I had little use for such techniques.

The relationship between throwing and groundwork is something like that between car wheels. When you use both in good combination, you should get a smooth ride.

From beginning to end I devoted my judo to winning. For this purpose I used my favourite techniques abundantly and developed combinations of techniques. I took an uncompromising stance right from the start in fighting for grips. I always tried to impose my own style on a fight.

Judo is a mental battle as well as a physical one. Whether it was an important competition or not, I concentrated on how to achieve perfection . In judo one has to be equally good mentally, physically and technically but I believe one's mental attitude is the most important factor.

COMBINATION 2 — THROWING TECHNIQUES TO GROUNDWORK

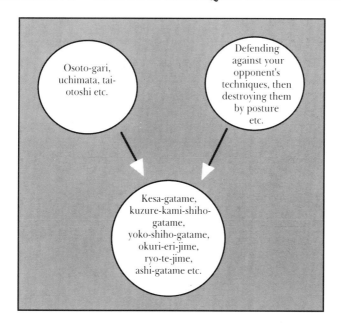

Nage-waza

CHAPTER 2

Osoto-gari

Celebrating an All-Japan championships win early in a long career.

Recollections of osoto-gari

My favourite technique is *osoto-gari*. Whenever I was in a win or lose situation, I used this technique, virtually without fail. When I did not use *osoto-gari* and lost I had no regrets. *Osoto-gari* is not a dabbler's throw, it is the finisher, the final clincher. To succeed with it you must have timing, confidence and total committement. However, there is a high risk of being countered if you make the slightest mistake. I remember when I was a first year at University I suffered a particularly bitter blow when I attacked a Polish player with *osoto-gari* and was spectacularly countered by *uranage*, which was a humbling experience. So, you have to be aware of this danger when you attempt *osoto-gari*. The crucial thing is to get the timing absolutely right.

Getting into osoto-gari

Osoto-gari was the first technique I learned. When I was at primary school I practised right *osoto-gari,* but in junior high school I changed to left *osoto-gari* and got my first *ippon* in competition with it. In my first dan grading examination I won every contest with *osoto-gari,* to get my black belt. I remember the first time I fought in the All Japan Championships at the quarter final stage I met Ishikawa and threw him for *yuko*, *waza-ari* and *ippon*, which made a big impression on me. The main reason my *osoto-gari* was so effective was that I paid special attention to getting the timing just right, that was the secret of my success with it. However I cannot say I made *osoto-gari* 'my technique', I feel I never completely mastered it. In the later years of my career, I had many contests with Hitoshi Saito of Kokushikan University, who was a really strong opponent. I used to go all out for ippon with *osoto-gari,* when fighting Saito, but I never managed to throw him for *ippon* with it, which looking back is my one regret regarding *osoto-gari* in my contest career.

Osoto-gari 1

This is my standard osoto-gari starting from the basic position of right 'hikite' or pulling handgripping around the area of my opponent's left outer sleeve, and my left 'tsurite' or fishing hand on his right collar. I can attack with all my favourite techniques - osoto-gari, ouchi-gari and uchimata - from this same grip. It has been said that this ability to attack with different techniques from one grip is one of my major strengths.

Whether or not you can complete your osoto-gari successfully or not, very much depends on whether or not you can break your opponent's balance successfully. This breaking of balance is important for all techniques but especially in the case of osoto-gari which is easy to counter if you make a mistake. If you break your opponent's balance well or badly, it will make the difference between winning or losing. When you break your opponent's balance, do it so as to place all his weight onto the heel of the leg which you going to sweep away.

It is important to step in aggressively onto your pivot leg (stepping/right leg). Point the toes of your sweeping leg and to sweep right through (see photo).

1. Assume a left handed position.
2–3. Take a large step forward onto the pivoting right leg.
4. Prepare the sweeping leg as you step forward.
5–6. Make contact with your opponent's left leg in the area of his rear outside thigh. The toes on your sweeping leg should be extended straight out. At this time it is essential that your opponent's weight should be transferred to the heel of his left leg. Fish up with your left tsurite and pull down with your right hikite.
7–9. Making effective use of your hands and dropping your head, make strong body contact and sweep right through.

 4

 5

 6

 7

 8

Key Points

1) How to break your opponent's balance. Pulling your *hikite* (right) down and thrusting up with your *tsurite* (left), bend your opponent over backwards and force his weight onto his left heel.

2) The stepping leg
In order to throw your opponent to his rear, you have to step in so that your standing foot is level with your opponent's feet. Be careful that your feet do not face in an outwards direction. When you have stepped in, it is better if you place your weight on your big toe rather than your little toes and if your knee is facing slightly inwards towards your opponent.

3) You should not sweep using your heel, but rather direct force into the toes as you sweep. In order to do this, you should point the toes of your raised sweeping leg.
With this method of sweeping, not only is the sweep very strong, but it is also effective when your opponent has braced his legs and is resisting and you have to redouble your efforts to complete the sweep.

4) Point of contact
Sweep somewhere between the area directly behind your opponent's knee and the widest part of his calf. Defensively this is the weakest area.

Developing osoto-gari – uchikomi on the move

This is used to cultivate speed, especially in the driving leg. Stepping forward, drive into your opponent. Have your *uke* retreat as quickly as he can. This is my favourite method of *uchikomi*. Before a competition, I always used to warm up with this practice.

Uchikomi with three people

This form of *uchikomi* is for increasing the power of your *osoto-gari* by applying the strength of both sweeping and pivotal legs. Using all your power, you sweep straight through to completion. After you sweep, you should try to complete the technique with all your strength for about three seconds without letting your breath out. For me this last "push" is very important.

The effectiveness of this practice is greatly increased if your opponent does not lift the leg which is being attacked, but rather resists stubbornly.

Osoto-gari 2

1) Assume a left-handed stance. 2–3) Take a large step forward on the pivotal right leg. (The same as the first *osoto-gari*) 4) Prepare the sweeping left leg as you step in. 5–6) Sweep in the same general manner as *osoto-gari* 1, but thrust up under your opponent's chin with your left *tsurite*.

The transfer of balance and head position are related. For example, if the head comes forward you are vulnerable to a forward throwing technique. If the head goes back, you are vulnerable to a rear technique. Accordingly, when fighting a tall opponent, I would break his balance by pushing his chin up. This method is also effective against round, heavy opponents.

Against tall people, in order to unbalance your opponent's upper body press his elbow in to his side, and thrust up under his chin.

3

4

6

5

Osoto-gari 3

Osoto-gari 3

Osoto-gari 1 and 2 are both examples of the technique in action when your opponent is backing away from you, and you step in to complete the throw.
(In this case, your opponent rests his weight on his back leg.)

By contrast, in this *osoto-gari*, firstly, push your opponent. Then, seizing the opportunity presented when your opponent returns the push, you attack with *osoto-gari*. The timing for this variation is extremely difficult.

The point is to feint a step backwards as your opponent returns your push and then suddenly step forward in the opposite direction. In the instant that it seems your opponent's advancing foot will touch the *tatami*, complete the technique.

Contest Tips 1 : tsurite and hikite

In judo it is very important to know how to read your opponents and to break their balance. As the level gets higher, of course, this becomes even more important. In order to break someone's balance it is essential to master the use of your *tsurite* and *hikite*. A fault often seen in beginners is that they try only the basic form of a technique such as *osoto-gari* and there is often a complete lack of movement in both *tsurite* and *hikite*. In these cases, the opponent's balance is not in the least disturbed and the player cannot make a good attack. Generally, people who can execute techniques successfully are very good at using their hands properly.

Furthermore, in order to move your *tsurite* and *hikite* properly, you must use your wrist properly. And the correct wrist movement depends on the use of the fingers. It is very important to put strength into your little, ring and middle fingers and to grip hard. Be careful to relax your thumb when you grip, as a stiff thumb causes a stiff wrist. The use of your hands is one of the fundamentals of judo and is the key to winning or losing.

1-2.   Push your opponent, causing him to retreat.
3.   Your opponent having been pushed, decides to take a step forward with his left leg and return the push. At this time, normally, my right leg would be pressured and I would retreat a step. Feint this action.
4/5.   Step forward onto your right pivot leg, crossing your opponent's left leg just as he decides to step forward.
6.   Seize the opportunity afforded by the instant your opponent's left leg touches the *tatami*.
7-8.   Complete the technique.

Osoto-gari 4

• Key points

The method of breaking your opponent's balance and the movement of your pivoting leg.

In [2] break your opponent's balance by pushing up under his chin with your *'tsurite'* and pulling your *'hikite '* towards your own chest, thus twisting his body. As your head goes forward, quickly bring your pivotal leg into action.

6

1) Standing against the opposing grip.

2-3) Break his balance with your *tsurite* pushing up by the side of your opponent's chin and your *hikite* pulling to the side. (Cause his upper body to twist round to the left.)

4-5) Step in onto your right leg (supporting.) Compared with the step taken against an opponent of similar grip, you must be careful that the step is quite shallow.

6) At the same time as you sweep with your left leg, pull in your supporting leg. (The action of the pivotal leg is important, see main points 2-3.)

7-8) Complete the technique.

7

My *osoto-gari* is basically a technique for use in contest against opponents of similar grip, although there have been many occasions when I've fought opponents with opposing grips. With similar and opposing grips, the preparations are different and the final forms of the throw are mutually distinguishable. Therefore you cannot just practise the basic form of *osoto-gari*.

•Key points

In the case of a contest with someone of opposite grip the set up is conducted from a distance and you open up your opponent's body. Thus it is difficult to throw your opponent directly to the rear. Rather, you completely unbalance your opponent and go straight into *osoto-gari*. From there, as your head goes forward while sweeping strongly, pull in your supporting leg and throw.

8

Osoto-gari 5

The strong point of my judo was "seizing the moment", so pulling in opponents forcibly from above did not often feature in my contests. However, as an exception, in this *osoto-gari*, I throw by catching the belt from over the opponent's back. The defensive posture adopted by my opponent so as not to be thrown involves bracing both arms, lowering the head and pulling back. If your opponent adopts this position you will not be able to step in easily. In this sort of situation, this *osoto-gari* is effective. Even though it goes slightly against one's own theory and principles, it is necessary to make a forceful attack in this case because of your opponent's position.

4

5

Against an opponent with a defensive posture.

1-2) Against an opponent adopting a defensive posture, use your body (opening out to the side) and let go with your *tsurite* grip.
3-4) At the same time, take hold of the belt at the back, past the head and pull your opponent's body towards you.
5) Sweep him directly backwards.

• Key points

Figures 2 and 3 represent a very quick movement. At this point if you desist for a moment your opponent will realise straight away and at the point represented by figure 3 you could be countered with a technique such as *sukui-nage*.

Viewed from the opposite direction.

Osoto-gari 6

This combination from *ouchi-gari* to *osoto-gari* was my most commonly used form of attack. *Osoto-gari* is a technique which amounts to an attack at the instant your opponent retreats, so in the case of this combination, I first lightly attack with *ouchi-gari*, force my opponent to give way and instantly come in with *osoto-gari*.

In this case the role of the *ouchi-gari* is strictly to introduce the following *osoto-gari*.

If you enter too deeply with the *ouchi-gari* attack, the following connecting movement to *osoto-gari* is difficult and you may end up off balance yourself. It is very important that in a combination of techniques, by using your *tsurite* and *hikite* to good effect, you should make your opponent think that the first technique is the real attack. (i.e. throw a dummy.)

1-3) Feint with a light *ouchi-gari*.
4-6) As your opponent retreats step decisively forward.
7-10) Throw with *osoto-gari*.

The *ouchi-gari* to *osoto-gari* combination is a pattern in which you follow your opponent as he moves backwards. In contrast to this, this combination from *osoto-gari* to *sasae-tsuri-komi-ashi* involves a forwards/backwards swing, in which you make your opponent think that you are going to throw to the rear but surprise him by throwing to the front. This is a combination often used by those players who favour *osoto-gari*. Recently, Nagoya Ogawa of Meiji University and Japan Chuo Kyoba Society has been taking up this combination as his speciality.

1-3)   Exert pressure with your *tsurite* in order to make your opponent think you are going to try an *osoto-gari* so that he will form the appropriate defence. In order to maintain his balance your opponent will bend his upper body forward.

4-8) Change to *sasae-tsuri-komi-ashi* and throw. If your supporting foot   points slightly inwards it is easier to throw.

* Key Points

In figure 3, even as I am going in for the *osoto-gari*, I am thinking "I'll change to *sasae*".

In figure 5, with my *hikite* grip I push up my opponent's elbow and pull down with my *tsurite*. I push out my hips and with my left leg block my opponent's right leg. I get the feeling of twisting my opponent's body around. In addition, at this moment, I am preparing for immediate follow up into *osae-komi*.

Osoto-gari in competition

November 1982 against Saito in the final of the Jigoro Kano International Tournament, over 95 kg category .

Here, I am just attacking with my speciality - left *osoto-gari*. Saito anticipates the move and pulls his left leg back a step to defend against it. As a result, my left *osoto-gari* is too far out and is not successful. A characteristic of my *osoto-gari* is to bring up my right pivotal leg from here, but Saito is very large around the thighs and his stability is very good, so this also was not good enough. I couldn't unbalance his upper body with my hands either. With nearly any other opponent, I would have been able to demonstrate the power of my *osoto-gari* even from this position, but in this case I wasn't. In the end I won with right *kosoto-gari*.

November 1982 , against Yoshimi Masaki in the semi-final of the Jigoro Kano International Tournament in the open category.

At this point my pivotal leg is moving forward, my left *tsurite* has been brought up, my opponent is completely off balance and his weight is shifting to his left leg. Following this, using my right leg which I had pulled forward as a pivot, I completed the throw in my usual manner and scored *ippon*.

April 1984 against Yoshio Fujiwara in the semi-finals of the All Japan Tournament.

1) The moment when I decided to go for *osoto-gari*. My left *tsurite* is pushing up under my opponent's chin. Fujiwara withdraws his left leg to try and escape but I seal off this movement well and drive with my sweeping left leg.

2) At the same time as I move my pivoting right leg , 1, 2 steps forward, I break his balance using my hands, and just as he places all his weight on his left leg, I sweep it away. I am standing on the toes of my right supporting leg. In this position, you can get spring in the body.

3) I throw him beautifully straight backwards. The toes of the sweeping leg (left) are extended. This photograph is proof that I follow the sweep right through to the end.

November 1981 against Angelo Parisi of France in the quarter-finals of a tournament in Japan in the over 95 kg category.

1) I have just come in for *osoto-gari*. Parisi has released his left grip (*tsurite*) and is defending by pushing against my face. If my face had turned to the side as a result of this pressure, my strength would have been diverted towards that direction and over-all power would have been reduced by half. Among Japanese players, there is rarely anyone who conducts this sort of defence, but in a contest with foreign players, I have found that care is necessary as there are unforeseen attacks and defences. At this time, notwithstanding Parisi's push, my *hikite* and *tsurite* were working well and his upper body balance was disrupted.

2) This is my sweeping action

3) I sweep straight back and win by ippon. I am all over him. Even after throwing, I control my opponent's upper body so that I can move immediately into groundwork. If there isn't the tenacity to "cut off the root of breath", the technique becomes too wishy-washy.

Ideas that have sustained me

1. "Tenacity"

This is my favourite word. This is the tenacity never to give up to the last and never to leave anything half-done. I believe that how far one's natural strength can take you is decided by whether or not one has this tenacity.

In judo, on the spiritual side, three things are essential: concentration, fighting spirit and this tenacity.

2. "There are no certainties in competition."

Never breathe easy to the end.
Never despair to the end.
Your opponent is not as strong as you think.
Your opponent is not as weak as you think.

This means that even in a competition where there is an inequality in ability between you and your opponent, with something of this belief the match can be turned. By "to the end" I mean until someone scores with *ippon* or until the contest time runs out. In short this means having the self-discipline not to throw away the contest.

There are those who, after they have lost excuse themselves by saying "I was careless" or "I didn't think he or she was that strong", but underneath it all, the real reason they lost is that they did not have enough tenacity in competition. There are many cases where someone trains for a competition, sweating buckets, putting in a lot of time, and accumulating studies of various tactics, then through a slight carelessness, throws away all this effort and is left with only regrets.

Until the very last, you must never give up or be relaxed or careless.

3. "The Arts of Pen and Sword."

This is a phrase I heard all the time from my teacher at school. This phrase is very important to me. This is because it is most important that one makes an effort in both fields - " I can do judo *and* study with a little application". Practically speaking, when you become a member of society, if you don't have a basic academic education you will have difficulties.

If you are to make the most of the endurance which you have gained from judo when you move out of the *dojo*, study is very important. Furthermore, one could say that the mental attitude of a competitor to make as great an effort as you can in any situation is an attitude which need not be confined to judo. To excel in both arts is extremely difficult but if you have the above frame of mind I believe that the path will be cleared of obstacles.

At the start of a contest, facing the opponent with both hands raised high and wide, back straight.

Recollections of ouchi-gari

For me, *ouchi-gari* is not a win or lose technique like *osoto-gari*. It's a technique which carries the role of a connecting medium to other techniques. In brief, it is a refined and sober technique. I believe that thanks to this technique, the breadth of my judo was considerably expanded.

In junior high school I learned *osoto-gari* first. After that, we were taught combinations from this *osoto-gari* to *sasae-tsuri-komi-ashi* and then from *ouchi-gari* to *osoto-gari*. I say this so that you will understand that in my judo, *osoto-gari* is the heart of my combinations and *ouchi-gari*, right from the start assumed a supporting role. (see diagrams on page 58).

The point about the *ouchi-gari* to *osoto-gari* connection is that they both need the same timing, and you can go for one or the other without your opponent knowing which one. The set up for *uchimata* is similar. I also applied myself to being able to execute an *ouchi-gari* to *uchimata* combination using the same timing.

As the level of opponent in practice and competition becomes higher, one's own techniques are more widely studied and so one cannot get an *ippon* with a single technique. It becomes a matter of outwitting an opponent and using two or three techniques linked to your win or lose technique and being able to take up a chance of winning. In order to achieve this, it is absolutely necessary to have techniques which are linked to your "big" throw. It becomes necessary to have a technique with which to attack the opponent from the inside, in other words *ouchi-gari* or *kouchi-gari*. In my case it was *ouchi-gari*.

I used *ouchi-gari* in the two following ways:

1) *Ouchi-gari* into another standing technique.

2) Feinting with another technique then attacking with *ouchi-gari*.

In the latter case, it hardly ever results in an *ippon* score, so you should control your opponent well and immediately follow up with groundwork.

In developing a good *ouchi-gari*, my main problem was that I was very large, so when I swept my opponent's leg from the inside I had difficulty in opening up my body properly. In order to get this right, I repeatedly practised turning by myself against a wall.

This technique which attacks on the inside is effective against opponents who are bigger than oneself. When I was a student, at my university's Tokyo Students' Tournament, where I won my first competition, I managed to take a satisfactory *ippon* off my rival Yoshioka of Chuo university. Then in the semi-finals of the Los Angeles Olympics I scored a knock-down with *ouchi-gari* against del Colombo of France.

This is a basic *ouchi-gari* used when your opponent is backing away from you by bending the knee of the leg on which you are standing and lowering your centre of gravity. Close in against your opponent's so that your chest is against his. Then, use the rotation of your hips to sweep your opponent's leg from the inside. To get him off balance, pull your *hikite* to the side, with a feeling of pulling your hips in, and while reversing your wrist on your *tsurite* push your opponent's shoulder. The toes of your sweeping leg should inscribe the shape of a half-circle. This should be done without lifting the leg.

Quite often *ouchi-gari* does not score an *ippon* so it is essential that in stages 7 and 8 you should adopt a position from which you can instantly attack with groundwork.

1-3) From a left-handed stance, just when your opponent backs away, take a large step forward onto your left leg.

4-5) Bring your chest right up against your opponent, bring your right pivotal leg up to your left leg, drop your weight so that your hips are lower than your opponent's and apply your *hikite* and *tsurite* to unbalance him.

6-7) Rotating your hips, sweep your opponent's leg from the inner side.

Developing Ouchi-gari

(A) Uchikomi on the move.

Get your opponent to move backwards as quickly as possible and matching the speed, follow him to practise your *uchikomi*.

Through this practice, the speed of your following leg will be improved. Work on this method as with *osoto-gari*, in particular before a competition.

Contest tips 2   The importance of uchikomi.

Through *uchikomi* you can instil the form of the technique. It is very important that no matter how many times you do *uchikomi*, you always maintain the same form. At the same time, you can impress on the memory how to break your opponent's balance. Once you know the form you can then apply speed. It doesn't matter how good your form is, if you have no speed you will not throw your opponent. Then, as you develop power it is important to keep readjusting to make sure of the timing. Generally when doing *uchikomi*, many people put too much emphasis on the form. However, in order to acquire a technique which will be useful in competition, speed, power and timing are essential and I develop these assets by thoroughly going over my 'moving' and 'three person' *uchikomi*.

(B) Three person uchikomi

This is a form of uchikomi which is suitable for developing power in both the sweeping and supporting legs. Having totally controlled *uke* you sweep until you knock him down. Do not allow him to lift the leg being swept but rather have him resist stubbornly. You should have a feeling of "one more effort; one more effort".

Ouchi-gari 2

This is an *ouchi-gari* for use against tall, heavy or rotund opponents. As was explained in the *osoto-gari* section, if you push up your opponent's chin he will be vulnerable to a throw to the rear. In using this method, the most important point is the use of the *tsurite*. In this case, your chest does not meet that of your opponent as in *ouchi-gari* 1. Thus, there are two methods of unbalancing your opponent: you can unbalance the body or you can unbalance him by pushing his chin up and back. This type of *ouchi-gari* uses the latter method.

1-3) Take a large step forward onto your left foot just as your opponent retreats. This time, in contrast to *ouchi-gari* 1, keep your arms to your sides and do not open up your opponent's body. This is quite similar to the opening moves of a *kouchi-gari*.

4) Swivel on your right foot, bend at the knees to lower your centre of gravity and thrust up under your opponent's chin.

5-7) With a slight feeling of raising your opponent's leg, sweep.

91

Ouchi-gari 3

This is a form of *ouchi-gari* in which you skilfully manoeuvre your opponent into moving the way you want him to. As you are pulling your opponent around in front of you, you should not move your backwards but rather should attack with a circular movement. This technique can very quickly be seen for what it is.

4

5

6

1) From a normal stance.

2-3) Take a half-step to the front corner onto your supporting right leg and using both hands turn your opponent around to the left. If you turn him in short bursts his right leg will be forced to come out to the front.

4-6). At the instant your opponent's right foot looks as if it will touch the floor sweep and throw.

Ouchi-gari 4

This is an entirely different style of *ouchi-gari* from that used to attack an opponent of similar grip. Rather than sweeping, it's a technique in which one makes full use of the *tsurite* and throws by lifting the "sweeping leg". This is especially effective against opponents with opposing grips who are very large, very heavy or have a low centre of gravity. (With the legs of very heavy players if you attack in the normal way you cannot make an effective attack and in many cases the technique will not work.) Sometimes from this *ouchi-gari* I will change to a hopping *uchimata*.

1) Stand with opposing grips i.e. left-handed against right-handed.
2) Continuously moving your left foot slightly, step in onto your right foot. At this time, it is important to push up under your opponent's chin with your *tsurite* and to pull your *hikite* in towards your stomach in order to break your opponent's balance.

3) Having thoroughly broken his balance, with a feeling of driving towards his left leg.
4-7) Hop forward twice, lift your opponent's right leg with your sweeping leg and on the third or fourth hop, throw. your opponent will fall down from the side and you will end up in a position as if you were about to do a rolling breakfall

As more people started to study ways of fighting me, the number of opponents who started to hold underneath and lower than my grip and defend by locking their elbows increased. Against this sort of opponent I pulled up from a grip over my opponent's arm and used this *ouchi-gari*.

1) With an opposite grip, your opponent is holding you off with straight arms.
2) Not taking a deep grip on the collar, but keeping the armpit closed down, as I turn my own arm from the outside grip, I push my opponent's arm inwards using my left elbow and close it up. An opponent who is keeping his arms straight is quite strong so this action of the elbow-armpit connection is important.)

As you do this, your opponent will redouble his efforts to push you away. In this stage, the main point is to cause your opponent to tense both arms and legs. You may accomplish this by the fact that there are many people who not only tense their arms but their whole body and they lose all suppleness. In other words, if your opponent is like a stick of wood , it is very easy to throw him.
3) At that moment, release the strength in your *tsurite*.
4-6)Throw your opponent with this *ouchi-gari*.

96

Your grip is very important in contest. In other words, attaining your own grip is the primary condition for winning contests. To make a contest go your way, you mustn't lose the fight for grips. When you get to be a first class player, for example, even if you have lost your grip, in one moment's movement you can recompose yourself and attack with your technique. However, it's still not easy.

Whether fighting opponents of right-left or similar grips, I hardly ever lost the battle for my grip. The reason for this was partly because of my contest philosophy and partly because I always tried to get my grip first .

In order to get the first grip, you have to start with your hands forward. In other words, no matter how awesome the opponent, or how nervous you are, your hands should be forward because once you have your grip, you can start moving your opponent around.

The following is what I mean by positive grip-fighting.
Having an intention of luring your opponent into doing what suits you is one thing but apart from this sort of case, you should always act positively. There are two ways of grip fighting: That is you can grip in order to attack with your technique or you can grip in order to prevent your opponent from attacking. The former is positive and the latter is negative. When you are thinking of attacking it is important to contend positively for your grip and in no way to compromise.

On one occasion I was advised by my *sempai* in the national team that "If you obstruct or insist on certain grips in practice you will never progress very much". I was thinking about that myself at that time. In conclusion, I decided that my gripping would be for throwing opponents but that it was not my intention never to defend against an opponent's attack so I should block opponents' grips when necessary. My attitude was that as long as I maintained a feeling of "hands out in front" it was a good idea to fight for grips even in practice. This attitude paid off in competition.

In fighting for grips, it is a mistake to think only about yourself getting a good grip as your opponent will also be desperate to grip first. Therefore, practically, you should think about getting a grip good enough to be able to throw from. In competitions nowadays, you often see both players fighting for grips from beginning to end and only taking hold when there is an ideal opportunity. This is a great shame.

If I am getting about 60% of the grips in a contest and the opponent is getting about 40% great! If it is 50-50 that's OK but, if you are only getting 40% of the grips or if you are at a disadvantage, for example when your opponent has taken points already or when you are in the position of deciding the result of a team competition, you will have to fight and put in attacks by brute force. If you can't produce your techniques with an evenly-matched grip, then you should re-examine them. If you lose the fight for grips, you should plan on moving your opponent around, using your legs and regaining control of your posture very quickly. In grip-fighting, you usually should aim at not losing a positive posture.

Osoto-gari 6

Starting with the intention of throwing with *ouchi-gari*, feint an *osoto-gari*. The whole point with this combination is that you make your opponent think that you are going to attack with *osoto-gari*. However, in your own mind you intend to combine it with *ouchi-gari*, so although the step forward onto your supporting leg looks fairly shallow, you can make your opponent think that you are going for *osoto-gari* by the use of your *hikite* and *tsurite*. In order to get around your *osoto-gari*, your opponent will part his legs and adopt a defensive posture. Taking advantage of this moment, continue into *ouchi-gari*. The main point is to get your opponent to open up his legs.

1) From an opposing grip.

2-3) Step forward onto your supporting right leg not too deeply but enough to look as if you are coming in for an *osoto-gari*. Make your opponent think it will be an *osoto-gari* attack by the actions of your *tsurite* and *hikite*.

4) With your opponent adopting a defensive posture against the *osoto-gari* and spreading his legs, your sweeping leg changes to an *ouchi-gari* attacking position.

5-8) Throw with *ouchi-gari*.

Ouchi-gari in competition

April 1984 against Yoshimi Masaki in the semi-final of the All-Japan Tournament.

The photograph shows me just starting my *ouchi-gari*. I am pushing Masaki with my *tsurite* (left hand) and pulling him with my *hikite* (right hand). This is so that when his right foot is raised, I push him in the direction of his left foot and hopping, throw him with *ouchi-gari*. However, in this instance, as can be seen from the photograph, my sweeping leg was too high and I couldn't complete the technique properly.

In this photograph, Sato has adopted a defensive position by taking both my lapels and keeping his arms locked out. He is pushing into my chest from underneath my arms. I am pulling him up from over his arms thus causing him to inject even more strength into his upper body in order to defend. However, the more strength he puts into his upper body, the more he loses his suppleness and the more like a wooden stick he becomes. Then, I suddenly relax making the next movement possible and attack with *ouchi-gari*.

Because of Sato's defence we are quite far apart and the sweeping leg is therefore too high. But, because my opponent has extended his back and hips to full stretch and both his legs are like rigid poles, the technique is successful and I scored *ippon*.

October 1979 Against Kurihara Sato at the All-Japan Student Tournament over 95kg category.

100

September 1981. Against Grigory Veritchev of the USSR in the over 95 kg category final at the world championships in Maastricht.

This photograph shows a very rare occurrence among my *ouchi-gari* attacks because I am attacking holding onto both lapels of Veritchev's jacket. His grip is a *kenka-yotsu* grip and it is extremely difficult for me to get a grip with my *hikite*. Also Veritchev, in order to better defend, does not come around to stand in front of me. So, no sooner have I got hold of his collar than I pull in hard and unleash my *ouchi-gari*. Veritchev is defending by pushing into my body with his left hand but immediately after this photograph, I broke his balance to the side and threw him for *koka*. Veritchev immediately turned in on the attack but as he did so I moved into a *yoko-shiho-gatame* and held him down.

When attacking, the grip and the timing of the technique are important. When your opponent dislikes your grip and is defending strongly, it is necessary to seize any unguarded moment and attack strongly.

Uchimata

Walking onto the mat at the 23rd Olympic Games in Los Angeles in 1984 putting aside an unexpected accident in the form of a torn calf muscle and keeping a very stiff upper lip.

Recollections of uchimata

I learned *uchimata* after *osoto-gari* and *ouchi-gari* but it came from behind to become my speciality. I have almost no recollection of winning with *uchimata* in junior high school. As with *osoto-gari*, I learned to combine *uchimata* with *ouchi-gari*. My *uchimata* is best when used against *kenka-yotsu* grip opponents, especially foreign players.

On the Tokai University Judo Club European tour during my second year of High School, I discovered the power of *uchimata*. It being my first overseas contest I was quite nervous at first. In my first fight (in Moscow) there were no *tatami* but a system of mattresses and I had a very difficult fight. However, I just about managed a decent *uchimata* and from then on I was fighting in a state of ecstasy and in the end I won all my thirteen fights. (twelve with *ippon*). I was the only one in our team to win all my fights. I often used *uchimata* so it is only natural that this gave me great confidence. From that time onwards, in fights against foreigners I often won with *uchimata*.

If we classify *uchimata* generally, there is the 'drawing out' type and the 'diving in' form. My *uchimata* is the 'drawing out' type which draws the opponent out in front of you thus breaking his balance. Why would my *uchimata* be most effective against foreign players? I believe the reasons are as follows:

1) Many foreign players have very stiff groin joints.
2) Breaking the balance by drawing the opponent out to the front is effective as Europeans are more used to the 'diving in' form.
3) When you apply your *ouchi-gari*, foreigners try to take you backwards, especially in the old USSR. When they do this, their head drops and so it becomes very easy to change from *ouchi-gari* to *uchimata*.

I believe that against foreign players, the drawing out form is far more effective than the diving in form.

Such *uchimata* specialists as Tomio Sasahara and Hitoshi Sugai, both world championship players, also use this drawing out form.

Uchimata 1

This is the basic form of the 'drawing out' *uchimata* against an opponent with a *kenka-yotsu* grip. The point in photographs 2 and 3 is how to draw your opponent out well and break his balance forward so that he is on tiptoes on both feet. In achieving this, the use of your head is very important.

• Key points

Tsurite - From an inner grip, turn the wrist of your *tsurite* which is grasping your opponent's jacket. Raising your elbow, turn it upwards to open up your side. When you do this, your opponent's right arm is raised and his upper body unbalanced.

Hikite - Turn your wrist and stretch out your elbow. With this action you can open up your opponent's armpit and transfer his weight to his toes.

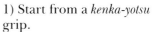

1) Start from a *kenka-yotsu* grip.

2) Drawing your opponent forward (see Key points)

3) Step forward onto your right supporting leg as your opponent's weight is coming onto his toes.

4) Step in decisively between your opponent's legs and onto your left leg.

5-8) Spring him up and throw.

Developing Uchimata

(A) Moving Uchikomi

In practising drawing your opponent forward it is very important that you break his balance very quickly. Therefore, in practice have him drag his weight backwards and concentrating on the use of your *hikite* and *tsurite* , draw him forward with your whole body making good use of your hips.

(B) Practising by yourself against a wall. (swinging your leg up).

After pulling your opponent forward, the leg swing becomes the deciding factor in the power of the technique. Accordingly with this practise one can practise the leg swing. It is also very effective as physical strength training for the supporting leg. Take care to point the toes of your leg as you swing it up. It is important to stand on the toes of your supporting leg. At any rate the swing should be high and decisive.

Uchimata 2   *While drawing your opponent forward*

Uchimata from an *ai-yotsu* grip is much more difficult than from a *kenka-yotsu* grip. If you just pull with the *hikite* it will be difficult to draw your opponent forward. Therefore, you should lure him forward little by little and just as he steps forward onto his left foot, come in for the *uchimata*.

1-3) Gripping in a normal position, lure your opponent forward.
4) I seize the chance afforded by the opponent stepping onto his left leg, as when he steps forward his weight is on his toes.
5-6) I spring him up with my left leg and throw him.

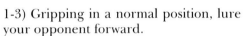

108

Contest tips 4 :   Movement

I mentioned the importance of grips and grip fighting in Contest Tips 3 but when it comes to throwing your opponent the most crucial factor is to break your opponent's balance and set up a throw. This is the point of *nagewaza* (throwing practice). Thus, the most important aspect of your training should be to acquire an effortless and efficient way of breaking your opponent's balance.

I was a heavy-weight player but I always aimed at matching the speed of the middleweight players especially when combining techniques such as *ouchi-gari* with *osoto-gari* or *uchimata*. I aim to destroy the opponent's balance while keeping the final technique uppermost in my mind. This is a characteristic of my judo which hasn't changed since my junior high school days.

If you let your opponent move as he pleases, in the end the contest will be at your opponent's pace. If this happens you will not be able to attack at will. For example, even if it only looks as if your opponent is moving more than you, in reality because you are luring him out, if you are eventually not moving at all, you will not be able to take the initiative in the contest.

Whenever I am fighting an opponent who is bigger or stronger than myself, and no matter how big he may be, he will always have a weakness, I am always determined to move my opponent around. I use foot sweeps, shake him up and then attack with my special throws. In the end, if this doesn't sap all his strength it can be a means of counter-acting his advantage in physical strength through movement.

In conclusion, the movement from technique to technique should incorporate breaking your opponent's balance, applying a fast technique before the opportunity is lost and then throwing him. This sort of movement is the key to winning or losing.

Uchimata 3

This combination from *ouchi-gari* to *uchimata* is my favourite combination. It has great power against opponents who have a very low centre of gravity, who have large physiques or who are very heavy. These opponents are difficult to raise with leg strength in a single attack. However, it is easy to lift a leg which your opponent has already raised in order to defend against an *ouchi-gari* attack. With this combination it is very important that the supporting leg be stable and in order to ensure this, training to strengthen the supporting leg is indispensable.

• Key Points

Use of the *hikite* and *tsurite*.
(See figures 5 - 8).
The main point is that the *hikite* pulls downwards.

1) Take a *kenka-yotsu* grip.

2-3) Lightly attack with *ouchi-gari*. There is no intention of throwing with the *ouchi-gari*, the aim being to cause your opponent to raise his leg to defend against it.

4) Step forward onto the supporting right leg. Pay attention to the direction of your toes. Pull your opponent off balance by pulling your *hikite* to the side.

5) Come in for *uchimata*. At this time in order to cause your opponent to lower his head, pull downwards with your *hikite* .

6-8) Break his balance further by pirouetting a half circle with your *uchimata* while pulling down further with the *hikite* and your opponent's head will go down. Then lift a second time (this is important).

9-10) Throw. Because I moved in a half circle after throwing him, my body is facing in the opposite direction.

Uchimata 4

This combination is effective against opponents who are lighter and more agile than myself. This variation is of particular use if you want to ensure that you are not countered with *uchimata sukashi*. This is because your opponent will take a step forward to avoid your *osoto-gari* and in doing so will take up a very open body posture from which position it is almost impossible to counter with *uchimata sukashi*. For *uchimata*, the wider your opponent spreads his legs the easier it is.

Combinations using osoto-gari as the pivotal technique

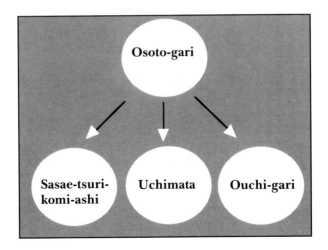

1) From a normal stance with a *kenka-yotsu* grip.

2-4) When you step onto your supporting leg and look as if you are going to attack with *osoto-gari*, your opponent will try to defend by sliding a step to the side and dropping his hips thus spreading his legs. Note that for light opponents the move to a defensive posture is very quick.

5) Quickly take advantage of the your opponent's change in posture.

6) As you change the direction of the toes on your supporting leg from that of *osoto-gari* to *uchimata*, twist your hips and take up position for the *uchimata*.

7-11) Raise him decisively on the right side and throw.

April 1981 Against Kaoru Matsui in the semi-finals of the All-Japan championship.

In this sequence of photographs, take note of the differences which signal the change of direction, especially the toes.

1). This is the outcome of a combination from *ouchi-gari* to *uchimata*. Matsui is defending well against my *uchimata* but, his head is already down and he is at the limit of his defences. A characteristic of my *uchimata* is to draw the opponent forward and cause him to lower his head like this.

2). As I pull him forward, I turn my body
well and throw him. Note again the angle
of the toes. If you turn well enough the
opponent will not be able to stop his body
from following. This attack resulted in an
ippon.

Ko-soto-gari

This was not a speciality of mine to the extent that I could get an *ippon* with it. However, as my techniques were all on one side (*ouchi-gari*, *osoto-gari* or *uchimata*) it was quite useful to have a technique in the opposite direction especially against opponents with a *kenka-yotsu* grip. Even if I didn't complete the technique well, it gave my opponent cause to think and at least taught him that my techniques were by no means all on one side. There are considerable benefits to be derived from confusing your opponent.

• Key points
1. Push your opponent's right elbow upwards. It is best to push it up with your fist. Shift your weight to your right leg. Pay attention to the position of the step you take on your left leg.
2. Quickly bring your supporting leg up to your sweeping leg.

1) In this case *uke* has a right grip to my left and his *tsurite* is gripping from below my arm. In other words, I am gripping over my opponent's arm onto the side of his collar. My *hikite* has a grip around his elbow.

2-3) As I step forward on my sweeping leg, I push up his elbow and his weight shifts to behind his right leg. It is important that your opponent should think that you are about to attack with *osoto-gari* from an *ouchi-gari*. This is so you can unbalance him to get him to position 3).

4) Bring up the supporting right leg to the sweeping leg.

5-7) Sweep him backwards with your left leg.

April 1980 Against Endo in the final of the All-Japan championship.

I am attacking with a left *kosoto-gari* from a *kenka-yotsu* grip. Endo is trying to escape backwards but I keep up the attack. He is fending me off fairly well by pushing under my right armpit with his right hand, and I cannot close the gap between us. However, at this time, I use my right hand to good effect and push up Endo's left shoulder. Owing to this action I got him well off-balance and managed to score *yuko*.

Recollections of Kosoto-gari

When I was fighting opponents who gripped on the opposite collar (*kenka-yotsu*) I always attacked with my *ouchi-gari* and *osoto-gari* by taking a step in on the left - always the same side. In cases where the opponent had a similar grip to mine (*ai-yotsu*) I had a technique for use on the other side – *sasae-tsuri-komi-ashi* - but, for *kenka-yotsu* opponents at first I did not have any such effective techniques. In other words a *kenka-yotsu* opponent need only look out for attacks from one side when fighting me and so it was very easy for them.

Therefore, I learned this technique in order to broaden my range of attacks. Even if I didn't do the technique well, I wanted to unsettle my opponents and make them think " I don't know whether Yamashita will come from the left or the right".

My main difficulty in acquiring a good *kosoto-gari* was that I did not grip deep on the collar, so fishing up the collar from above was not sufficient and I had problems getting the timing right. Accordingly, it was quite late in my career when I first started to use this technique. I recall it being about the third year of university.

The first time I used this technique to any effect in a big competition was in my fourth year of university in the final of the All-Japan championship against Endo in 1979. The following was written in the tournament write-up in the magazine "Judo" published by the Kodokan.
"....... Four minutes having elapsed, Endo, retreating in the face of Yamashita's left

ouchi-gari tried to turn it into a right *uchimata* to no avail. Yamashita tried a left *osoto-gari* but Endo braced his right arm and wasn't moved. Then, Yamashita *attacked with left kosoto-gake* and Endo went down almost outside the area (*yuko*).

After that I took a *waza-ari* with a left *ouchi-gari* and held him down with *kuzure-kami-shiho-gatame* but I believe that if I hadn't shaken him up with that *kosoto-gari* (gake), I wouldn't have been able to break through Endo's defence.

Then, in my last All-Japan championship in 1985 in the quarter finals, in a teacher/student showdown with Toikawa I knocked him down with this *kosoto-gari* and held him for *ippon* with *yoko-shiho-gatame*. At this rather late stage in my competitive career I realised the important role which *kosoto-gari* has in combination with groundwork.

The difference between *kosoto-gari* and *kosoto-gake* is that in *kosoto-gari*, you sweep your opponent's foot with your foot whereas in *kosoto-gake*, making the sole of your foot the centre, you hook his leg and charge into your opponent. When you start your technique, you may be meaning to sweep with a *kosoto-gari* but depending on the timing and impetus of the technique, it might end up as a *kosoto-gake*.

To sum up, my *kosoto-gari* did not have the power for me to say "I can score *ippon* with this technique". Rather, it was at the fringe of my studies of means of fighting opponents with *kenka-yotsu* grips and was taken on only out of necessity.

Tai-otoshi

Tai-otoshi is a rhythm and timing technique. If, in pulling up , dropping both hands and in extending the knees, you do not fully coordinate the movement in your hands, hips and feet, you will not be able to apply this technique. Within all this, the point is how to draw your opponent off balance to the front. I practised this technique due to the necessity of fighting very large players. On these occasions, I paid special attention to drawing the opponent forward.

•Key Points.

The main point is to how to draw your opponent forward properly. Accordingly, how you turn your wrist is important as can be seen through looking at No. 4 from a different angle.

5

1-3) Pull your opponent forward and rotating your right leg, which will be the pivotal leg, place it behind the heel of your left leg
4) As you turn up the wrist of your *hikite*, pull *uke's* body strongly forward as if you were lifting it out of water, and pivoting on your right leg open out your body.
5) Step in front of your opponent's left leg as it comes forward. The direction of your toes should be the same as those of your *uke* and both knees should be slightly bent. Your weight should be evenly distributed on both legs (towards the big toes).
6-8). Push your left hand up and as you extend your knees, describe a big circle out and down with both hands, spring and throw. As you throw and while rolling, it feels as if you carry your opponent on your back.

6

7

8

Recollections of tai-otoshi

In August 1974 I left Kumamoto and made up my mind to go to Tokyo. Through this move I was able to see the world beyond Japan. Up until then I had thought that at 180 cm tall and 126 Kg I was quite big. Certainly I was big within Japan but the first thing I discovered about this new world was that I really wasn't that big. There are many players who are bigger and heavier than me. Could I really use my techniques based on *ashiwaza* such as *osoto-gari* and *uchimata* on their own, against these bigger opponents? This was one wall I ran up against.

As a measure to solve this problem, I resolved to acquire "carrying' techniques. Happily in Tokai university there were experts such as Inokuma *sensei* (*ippon-seoi-nage* and *tai-otoshi*) and Sato *sensei* (*tai-otoshi*) to call upon and I soon received guidance in *tai-otoshi* from these teachers. Then, under their tutelage, and being buffeted along the way by the many *sempai* aiming to become world class players, I sweated my way to acquiring *tai-otoshi*. However, the timing for this technique is very difficult and even piling practice upon practice, I couldn't get the body control I wanted. In the end it was good for nothing.

Accordingly, I rarely used this technique in competitions. However one competition which stands out in my memory was the Kano Cup in November 1978 when in the semi-finals of the over 95 kg category against Jean-Luc Rougé of France, I won with a *tai-otoshi* into a hold-down. Then seven years later in 1985 in my last All-Japan championships, I produced an instinctive *tai-otoshi* against Masaki in the semi-finals. That year, my physical condi-tion was poor and I had been thrown twice with *ouchi-gari* in the competition training three months before, by Masaki. To make things worse we were on live television... anxieties rushed around my head... if I can't win this I might as well give up I thought as I went onto the mat. I believe that this change in feeling con-tributed to my success. In this do-or-die situation my *tai-otoshi* perfected over long years of practice came naturally. Because Masaki wasn't expecting anything like my *tai-otoshi*, it probably took him by surprise. Having thrown him forward I held him down with my speciality – *yoko-shiho-ga-tame*. In the end I was saved by the tech-nique which I couldn't get right since I started learning it in the second year of high school.

April 1985 Against Masaki Yoshimi in the semi-finals of the All-Japan championships.

Sukui-nage

When you are being gripped from over the arm in an *ai-yotsu* grip, your head is lowered and it is difficult to execute any sort of technique. In this situation, when your opponent attempts to throw, reply with this *sukui-nage*. In practice, it was very rarely that anyone took an *ai-yotsu* grip over the top in a competition and so I had very little opportunity to use *sukui-nage*. However, having this technique, even if an opponent reached over and my head was pushed down I was in no haste and could survey my options. It was very advantageous having this technique under my belt.

124

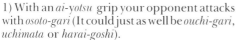

1) With an *ai-yotsu* grip your opponent attacks with *osoto-gari* (It could just as well be *ouchi-gari*, *uchimata* or *harai-goshi*).

2-3) Pull your left leg back and assuming a defensive posture, block your opponent's attack while maintaining your balance. As you drop your hips, insert your left hand between *uke's* thighs from behind.

4-5) With a feeling of sticking your stomach out, pick your opponent up. Your hips should be lower than his and it is with your hips that you pick him up, not with your arms.

6) Quickly push your right hip in, raise your right hand (between his legs) and pull down on your *tsurite*.

7-8) Your opponent turns nicely over as you throw to the front.

Tani-otoshi

This technique generally involves breaking your opponent's balance to a rear corner from a defensive position and throwing him backwards. However, in my case, I learned it as a technique for use against opponents who have a deep *kenka-yotsu* grip and pull you in close. The major point about this throw is that you must immediately follow up into groundwork.

•Key Points

1. The first stage is to defend properly against *uke's* attack by pushing your hips out. Then you can pull him in close. As you make progress, you will be able to pull your *uke* in close even as you make your defence.

2. Break your *uke's* balance forward as in figure 4, then skillfully use the power of his reaction.

3. When he is down, you must make sure of a hold-down. There is more of a feeling of dragging your opponent down backwards rather than throwing him.

1). *Kenka-yotsu* gripping. *Uke* is pulling in from above.

2). *Uke* attacks with *harai-goshi* (or *osoto-gari* or *uchimata*). From a defensive position, thrust your hips forward and defend againsts his throw. At the same time, pull his hips nearer with your left hand. This is in order to straighten out his hips).

3). *Uke* lowers the leg he was going to sweep with (his right leg).

4). Break his balance forwards. If you do this, *uke* will try to shift his weight backwards in order to counter this action .

5) Use the power of this backwards movement and with your hips still close to your opponent's, extend your left leg and sweep both his legs from behind.

6/7). Push him down to the rear corner. It is very rare that you will get an *ippon* from this throw.

8) Hold him down in *yoko-shiho-gatame*.

Ukiwaza 1

This is a throw which pulls the opponent forward in response to your opponent having an *ai-yotsu* grip and taking a deep grip on the collar from over your arm. Therefore you should be decisive with your *hikite*.

1) When you get a solid grip just under your opponent's elbow with your *hikite*, *uke* will stiffen his arm in order to defend. Using the strength of this reaction, pull him forward.

2-3)) Step forward on your left leg towards your opponent's advanced left leg, pull sharply with your *hikite* (right hand) and with your *tsurite* (left) push and twist in the region between shoulder and chest and cause your opponent to move slightly to the side. Throw your own body, fully exerting your *hikite*.

4) *Uke's* left leg will hit your right leg around the inner part of your knee. as he is twisted over.

5-7) Throw him diagonally up to the right hand corner. You should always follow the movement of your opponent and if there is a chance, change to *osaekomi* immediately.

Ukiwaza 2

When your opponent has a *kenka-yotsu* grip, sweep his legs aiming at the forward left leg.

•The feeling of each throw is rather different.

1) This throw has the feeling of twisting your opponent around on the pivot of his own legs.

2) Here, the feeling is more of knocking your opponent flat from in front, straight down onto the *tatami*. This sometimes causes injury to the shoulder so you should pay attention to your *ukemi*.

1) With a *kenka-yotsu* grip each has hold of the other's sleeve. The *tsurite* (left hand) is around the area from the shoulder to the chest.

2) Stepping forward slightly on your right leg, pull your *hikite* forward.

3) Place your right leg outside *uke's* right leg, timing it just as he step forward.

4) Place your right leg so as to sweep uke with your calf or achilles tendon, just as he tries to step forward. (your opponent will feel as if his face is going to dive into the *tatami*.)

5) Close up the armpit on your *hikite*. This makes for a position by which your opponent will hit the *tatami* with his shoulder.

6-8) Throw him diagonally towards the right corner. In the same manner as *ukiwaza* 1, you should follow his line of flight.

Recollections of Sacrifice Throws

My weak point used to be when I was being pulled in close from a grip over my arm by an opponent with a *kenka-yotsu* grip. When I got into this position, I would lower my head and not be able to produce any attacks. I was driven by necessity to learn a technique as a counter-measure and I learned the sacrifice throw *tani-otoshi*. It is fair to say that I didn't learn it so much as end up learning it. It's a technique that came naturally. That was just before I took the All-Japan championship title at the age of nineteen.

The acquisition of *tani-otoshi* goes along with progress in groundwork techniques. At that time, I was quite confident in groundwork, for example, I thought that even if I didn't do a *tani-otoshi* skillfully, it would be alright if I held the opponent in the position in which he had fallen. Sacrifice throws are, as the name implies, techniques which involve throwing your own body. Therefore if you get the timing or method wrong, it can be suicidal as there is a distinct possibility that you would end up being held down by your opponent. In other words, if you have no confidence in groundwork, you will inevitably hesitate to use this technique. Confidence or lack of it, can heavily influence the way in which you attack with this technique. On this point, through my proficiency in groundwork, I had confidence that even if my *tani-otoshi* were not to be decisive, I could follow up into groundwork.

Furthermore, as a by-product of acquiring *tani-otoshi*, your opponent will be looking out for it and will not grip over your shoulder. This fear of being countered by *tani-otoshi* can give you a distinct advantage against players whose speciality is gripping in this manner. And so, through this technique, I overcame my greatest weakness. Far from feeling technically stifled, on the contrary, I came to like opponents who gripped over my arm with a *kenka-yotsu* grip. I was able to turn my weakness into a strength by using *tani-otoshi*.

Amongst the sacrifice throws, I also used *ukiwaza*. I did not use this technique more than once in a contest but in practice could demonstrate its power and form. I developed this technique through the encouragement of Sato *sensei* who as he entered the latter half of his career as a player was already number one in Japan and the world.

At the time, I lacked the will to come to grips with new techniques. I had lapsed into a kind of routine. With this attitude, even though Sato *sensei* advised me "It would be a good idea to learn this technique as a surprise for Saito", I didn't take it to heart and decided that it would not be a good throw for me with my stiff hips. I told *sensei* "It's not for me!" Of course Sato sensei was rather annoyed and he ended up scolding me. " I advised you with **you** in mind. If all you can do is complain then there's nothing I can do. Being able or not able to do it is beside the point. The important thing is to have a go."

I didn't realise that I had lost the readiness to accept advice. With my succession of wins, I perhaps naturally became presumptuous. This happens even if one is self-disciplined. There is nothing so dangerous for development as an inflated ego.

Eventually, the proficiency of my *ukiwaza* got to the level where it became a natural response during practice sessions. As for not using it in competition, my usual style of judo is to attack and it doesn't suit that sort of approach.

April 1982. Semi-final of the All-Japan Tournament against Nobutoshi Hikage

My opponent has attacked with an *osoto-gari*. Just as he has done so, I have turned to his rear, wound around him and thrown him straight back with *tani-otoshi* for a *yuko*. Then I followed up into groundwork. While throwing your own body, it is important to drag your opponent down. It's not really like throwing him.

Katame-waza

Being thrown up and down by my team-mates and coach on achieving my dream of an Olympic gold medal in Los Angeles in 1984.

Katame waza: groundwork techniques

Opening my eyes to groundwork techniques.

In both Fujien Junior High School and Kyushu Gakuin High School, I was a standing technique player. I was not really a *newaza* (groundwork) specialist. Even at Tokai University, I was secure enough in standing practice, but when it came to *newaza* , that was the bad part. At the start of a *newaza* session, the cries of my *sempai* rang out from all points of the *dojo* "Oi Yamashita". However, one day an astonishing thing occurred. This could be called my "Conversion to *newaza* ".

One day when practising with Sato *sensei* - feared throughout the world of judo as being the best *newaza* practitioner in Japan –I managed entirely by chance to apply a stranglehold. (see chapter one - contests). Every day in Sato *sensei's* special *newaza* lessons I was mercilessly held down, strangled, armlocked and I had finally managed to come up with response to these onslaughts, but I never dreamt that I would beat Sato *sensei*! Through this one fortuitous incident, I soon became much more confident in *newaza*. This stemmed from an extremely simple concept that made sense to me at the time: " I beat Sato *sensei* so there is no reason for me to lose to anyone else." With hindsight, I could say that unconsciously, *newaza* was hammered into me by the rough training that Sato *sensei* put me through.

If we try and compare standing and ground techniques, it is natural to become somewhat predisposed to standing work as it takes a long time to become adept at a throwing technique. On the other hand, it is possible, with effort, to improve your skill at groundwork in a comparatively short time.

The old pre-war colleges, were famous for their *newaza* and when you think that those colleges' judoka devoted all their enthusiasm to *newaza* training with the attitude that "The quantity of training is all-important" you feel that they understood the merits of *newaza*.

Shinguma *sensei* who was apprehensive of the fragility of bravery, relates the significance of the rather easily understood *newaza* in this extract from "The Essence of College Judo" -

"Standing and ground work are two sides of one body and are like the wheels of a chariot. When the contest is undecided, your arms and legs are tired out, you aren't up to it and yet you must get a result, there is nothing for it but to use newaza. In these cases you can fully realise the importance of newaza."

Through having confidence in my *newaza*, I was able to develop great breadth to my judo, centred as it was on standing techniques. Moreover, in the latter half of my career as a player when I was physically past my peak, *newaza* became even more important and through it I was frequently able to escape from dangerous situations. The best example of this was in the Los Angeles Olympic Games when I tore my calf muscle in the second round and I still shudder to think what would have happened if I hadn't had my *newaza*. People do not talk about my judo without including *newaza*. My judo is supported on the 2 wheels of standing and ground techniques and demonstrates it's power through that combination.

The Los Angeles Olympics: the power of newaza

In the second round, I injured my leg when attacking Schnabel (West Germany) with *uchimata*. I pretended to be calm, crushed his seoi-nage attempt and took the contest with *okuri-eri-jime*. (2 minutes 50 seconds). In the third round, del Colombo of France got a *koka* with an *osoto-gari*. This was the first time I had ever been thrown by a foreign player. It was a great shock but I pulled myself together, knocked him down with an *ouchi-gari* (*waza-ari*) then held him with *yoko-shiho-gatame*. (2 minutes 10 seconds). In the final against Rashwan of Egypt he quickly attacked with *harai-goshi* but I automatically opened up my body and making space, destroyed the attempt; then immediately attacking with *newaza* I held him with *yoko-shiho-gatame*.
I held on telling myself that even if an earthquake were to flatten the hall, I would complete the hold. (1 minute 5 seconds).

Kesa-gatame

The word "*kesa*" in *kesa-gatame* refers to a traditional piece of clothing worn by priests around their necks. This technique seems to be easy but there are points in it which are difficult to get right. Placing your weight, getting your balance and responding to your opponent's movements are all difficult. In my case I made good use of my heavy weight.

• How to grasp the lapel.

From underneath your opponent's right armpit, push your left hand in and grasp your opponent's left lapel.

1) Move around to the right side of your opponent. Insert your left hand under his right armpit. Grip his left lapel with your fingers inside. This is an important detail. At that point, it is important that you put pressure on your opponent by resting your weight on him.

2) Take your opponent's left sleeve with your right hand.

3) As you take your weight off your opponent, pull his sleeve diagonally forward thus extending his body.

4) Pull your right hand in towards your own body, make close contact with your opponent, (you should be chest to chest) and apply your weight well.

5-6) As you push your right leg forward, turn your opponent over and hold him down with *kesa-gatame*.

• Key points.
1. Do not separate your hips from the side of your opponent's body.
2. Maintain close upper body contact and control your opponent's left arm properly by placing it firmly under your armpit.
3. Keep your balance well by using both legs to good effect.

Yoko-shiho-gatame

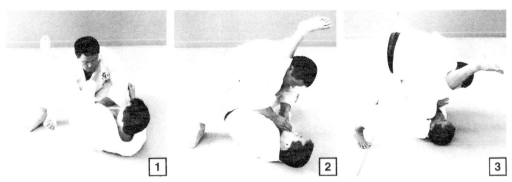

As a response to an opponent who was pulling me in from a position on their back, I most often used this form of *yoko-shiho-gatame*. It is an effective sort of attacking technique for those who are heavy and very strong.

1) *Uke* is pulling you towards him from underneath so that you are sandwiched between his legs. In this situation, push your right hand under his left leg from the inside outwards in order to get his leg onto your shoulder. With your left hand catch hold of his left lapel.

2) Keeping close contact between your body and his legs, manoeuvre so that his leg is on your shoulder.

3) With the hand that is supporting uke's leg (your right hand) take a deep hold with an over-grip on the right hand side of the nape of his neck. At this time, it is important not to let *uke* raise his back off the floor too much as he may try to roll backwards and escape.

4) Control your opponent's left arm with your right knee so that he doesn't turn out of the hold.

5-8) Pushing *uke* forward, hold him down with *yoko-shiho-gatame*. I usually maintain close body contact with my opponent especially in the area of the abdomen. At stage (6) if you can, take his right arm across under his back with your left hand, and he will not be able to move to free his arm.

Contest tips 5 : Attack and defence with groundwork techniques.

If we classify groundwork attacks and defence from the point of view of attack, we can make a great distinction between attacks from on top and those from below. If groundwork is combined with throwing techniques, attacks from on top are overwhelmingly predominant. Attacks from below are technically possible, but under present regulations, to abruptly pull someone down into groundwork is against the rules, so you have to take care. The characteristics of my groundwork are as follows:

1) I always attack from on top, from which position I can make full use of my weight. Groundwork from below is not suited to my body shape so I don't usually do it.

2) I pay serious consideration to following up from standing techniques into groundwork.

3) I look for the winning hold and pursue certainties. In other words, my groundwork is "to the end". "Yamashita's groundwork" does not include all groundwork. Even for ground-work techniques it is important to build up patterns best suited to yourself like this.

• Key Points

Attack and defence. (See picture 1.)

A......In order not to let his leg be hoisted onto your shoulder, your opponent will try to stiffen and defend with that leg. In this case use your opponent's bracing force, drop his left leg, control it with your right knee and, moving your whole body to the right, attack from your opponent's left side.

B......If your opponent should suddenly roll over his shoulder and escape... allow him to turn, then when he is on all fours, attack him in that position.
(See the next page)

Okuri-eri-jime

In many cases when I practised groundwork, with the opponent on all fours I attacked from behind or to the side. The most often used technique was this *okuri-eri-jime*. You could say that this technique is the pivot or centre of my groundwork.

1) Starting on the right of your opponent, grab his left wrist with your left hand, press down on his right shoulder with the right side of your chest.

•Key points• 1

Push down on his right shoulder and rest your weight on him in order to control the movement of his right arm.

2) Confine his movement further by catching his right leg with your left one. Otherwise he may be able to roll out of your attack and counter-attack with *ushiro-kesa-gatame*.

3) Push your right hand in over his arm and take a deep hold on his left lapel.

4/5) Trying not to open up your armpit, strangle your opponent.

•2.

In pictures (1) and (2) it is quite difficult to get hold of your opponent's left wrist. your opponent will try to counter-attack by clamping your left arm (which you pushed in to take his wrist with) under his armpit and rolling you into *ushiro-kesa-gatame*. In order to guard against this, first of all you should take your opponent's right leg with your own left leg. By doing this you make it impossible for your opponent to roll. Whether or not you do this is the key point of this technique.

Contest tips 6 : How do you finish it quickly?

With a follow-up from a throw into groundwork it is important that you do it 'in the twinkling of an eye'. In a competition, there aren't all that many chances to win but there will definitely be one or two. That chance often comes when your opponent's posture has been disrupted by his attempt at a throw. You mustn't let the chance pass.

What should you do in order not to lose the few instances when your opponent's defence is down? The only way is to make the actions come automatically to your body through continual practice. In other words, in everyday practice, you should not practise in a slipshod manner thinking "It's only practice". Furthermore, it is wrong to neglect the follow-up into groundwork because you think "If I get *ippon* with a good throw, *that* would be good". Usually, the times when you penetrate your opponent's defence and win a contest are brought about by accustoming your body movements through continual practice with a mental attitude of " I will finish it quickly and surely!" Thus, decision on whether to apply a holddown, strangle or armlock will come automatically to your body in response to a situation.

Strangling:7 key points

1

You may say that for someone like me with thick arms and big hands to have a strangle as my speciality is rather rare. A characteristic of my strangle techniques is that when I strangle I make good use of my heavy body. This is one of the important points.

Scoop up your opponent's right arm. (Pictures 1 and 2.) With your opponent defending, insert your left hand under his left armpit and grabbing his left hand, put it out of commission.

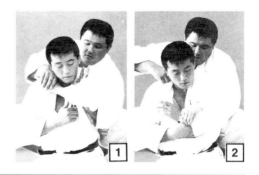

2

1) Poke your fist in along your opponent's neckline.
2) Take as deep a grip as possible on your opponent's left collar.
3) Turn your wrist and strangle. You do not strangle with the jacket but rather with your wrist.

 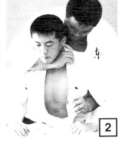 

3

If your opponent tries to defend by preventing you from getting his collar...
1) If he pulls with his left hand he will easily break your grip on his collar.
2) In order to avoid this, slide your hand along the neckline of his collar very quickly and get your right hand in under his chin.

4

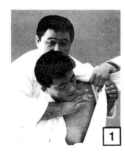

If your opponent defends by preventing you from getting the collar....
1) When you attempt to strangle, your opponent defends by pulling his own left collar away. If this happens, grasp his collar with your left hand just below his hand.
2) Push your hand firmly inwards. As you do this, you will easily be able to get a grip on the collar with your right hand and continue the technique.

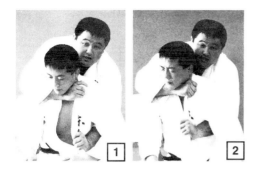

If your strangle is loose and you cannot finish your opponent off... Pull down on your opponent's left lapel with your left hand and take up the slack in his *gi*.

5

6

6 If your opponent defends against the advance of your strangling hand into his collar by putting in his own right hand...

1) Make a space between his right hand and neck by pushing his hand down with your left hand. The space should be made at the point where his elbow contacts the right side of his chin.

2) Following the line of his chin, quickly insert your hand down the right side of his head and push your left hand in under his left armpit.

3) Working your hand under his right wrist, take a deep grip on his left collar.

4) Grip the right lapel with your left hand and pull it downwards. Turn your left wrist out and strangle.

7

7 If at the beginning of the example shown in No. 6, your opponent's right hand defence is shallow, slide your right hand in **over** his right hand and gripping his collar, strangle.

145

(A) To kuzure-kami-shiho-gatame

1) Position yourself on the right hand side of *uke* who is on all fours, for an attack with *okuri-eri-jime*. Put your left hand in under his armpit and take hold of his arm. Do not hold onto anything with your right hand. At this time, *uke* will defend and the feeling will be of him turning to the right so as not to be strangled.

2-3) Put your weight onto is right shoulder and roll him to the right with his head as the fulcrum.

4-5) From this position apply *kuzure-kami-shiho-gatame*.
    The key points are 3,4 and 5 and to keep your arm close to your opponent.

(B) To yoko-shiho-gatame

1) Starting from the same position as (A), grasp *uke's* collar with your right hand, put all your weight on his back and strangle.

2) *Uke* will drop onto his left shoulder, pull in his chin and roll to the left to try and escape the strangle.

3-5) Making good use of *uke's* rolling movement, as you make close body contact with your chest, pour all your weight onto him and hold him down with *yoko-shiho-gatame*. In this one long movement, at stage 3) you should guard against getting your legs caught up while trying for a hold-down, so it is important for you to put your left knee in his left side.

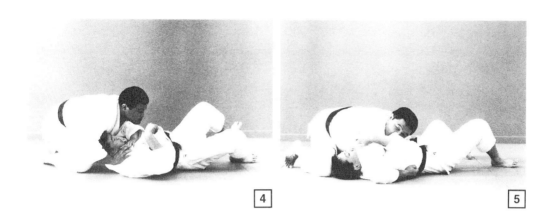

4 5

I often used *kuzure-kami-shiho-gatame* and *yoko-shiho-gatame* as combinations from *okuri-eri-jime*. In these cases, an important point is that with the idea from the beginning that you will try to finish him off with *okuri-eri-jime*, your opponent will defend against the strangle desperately and you will be able to make good use of a moment created by that defence action. It is best if you can decide the contest with the first *okuri-eri-jime*.

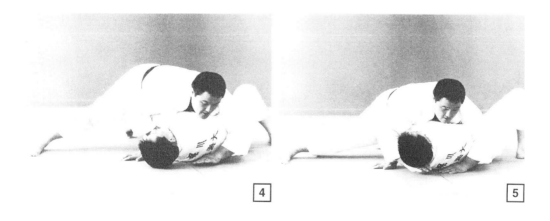

4 5

From strangles to holds

From okuri-eri-jime to yoko-shiho-gatame - seizing the moment when he tries to escape the strangle

1) With your opponent flat on the floor, sit on top of him as if on a horse.

2-3) Slide your left hand under his left armpit and grasp his wrist. At the same time, bring all your weight to bear on his back and both arms. If your opponent is large the arms don't move even though they are bearing your combined weights. If your opponent is small, there should be an effect when you apply your weight.

Depending on the case, push your opponent forwards.

 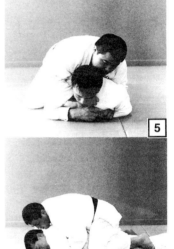

4-5) Go in for *okuri-eri-jime*.

5) A view from the side.

The method of attacking someone who is flat out is the same as that used when attacking someone on all-fours. First make a solid attack with *okuri-eri-jime* and try to score *ippon*. When you do this, your opponent will turn his attention to his defence against the strangle and in that moment there will be a chance to turn him over for a hold-down. Don't lose the chance and make good use of your weight to hold him down. The main point is that you can hold the *okuri-eri-jime* secure right up to the end.

148

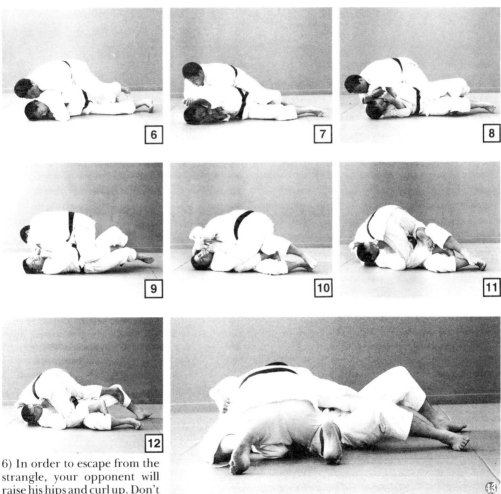

6) In order to escape from the strangle, your opponent will raise his hips and curl up. Don't let this opportunity pass, but entwine your left leg around his left leg, thus preventing him from being able to go back to the left hand side.

7) Scoop his armpit up a bit more with your left hand and clasp your hands together behind his head.

8-9) Push his head to one side. As he cannot return to the left, he has no choice but to face upwards.

10) First get a firm hold on the upper half of his body. In 9, 10 & 11 pay attention to how you use your left knee. Sometimes your knee is pushed down and your leg caught up by your opponent. In order to prevent such a situation, you should keep your knee close to his right side.

11) When you have made sure of the upper body, completely free your left leg using your right leg to help .

12) Hold down with *tate-shiho-gatame*.

13) You can change your hold to *yoko-shiho-gatame* from if necessary.

Ashi-gatame

This technique is favoured by heavy players. I increased my groundwork power by making this my speciality. Even in the All-Japan Tournament I used this from the beginning and was effective with it. In instances such as when your opponent tries a throw and is crushed, and when he is on all-fours, there is a chance to apply this technique. It is important not to miss your chances.

1) Your opponent being on all-fours, come around to his right side, insert four fingers into the back of his collar and push his head down lightly. As a reaction to being pushed your opponent should raise his head slightly.

2) Use the momentum of your opponent lifting his head, pull up his upper body so his armpit is exposed and in that instant catch his right arm with your right leg.3) Trapping his wrist with your right heel. extend his arm.

•Key points (A)
1] Push his head down
2] Use his reaction to pull him upwards. Also pay attention to how you hold he jacket with your right hand.

• Key points (B)

How to get hold of his arm with your right leg.

Lead with your heel!

4) Press down on your opponent's right shoulder and crush him. The crush
   should be perfectly placed rather than being a matter of strength alone.
5) Thrusting out your abdomen, the armlock will go on when you lift your
   legs.

If your opponent has very flexible joints or if your attempt at an armlock is too loose....

4-6) Keeping his right arm caught up by your right leg, slip your left hand in
   under his armpit and grasp his left wrist thus gaining control of both his
   arms.
7-8) Strangle him with *okuri-eri-jime* using your remaining right hand.

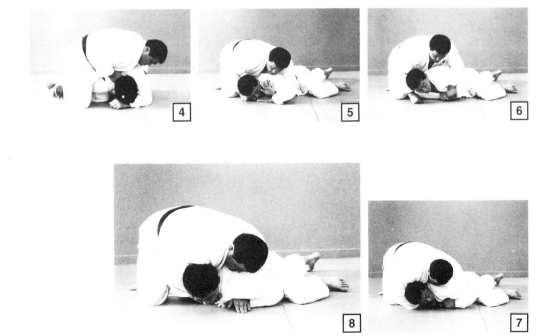

Catching the arm: basic practice

As a counter

At times when your opponent has come in for a throw such as *ippon-seoi-nage* but has not broken your balance sufficiently and falls on his knees into a position on all fours, there is a golden opportunity for *ashi-gatame*.

1) Your opponent's technique fails.
2) As he goes immediately to all-fours in defence..
3) Catch his right arm with your right leg.

Dealing with flexible joints

In the case of photograph 4 on page 151, if you attack with *ashi-gatame* and your opponent has very flexible joints, the armlock will not work. In this case you should use this method of rearranging the arm.

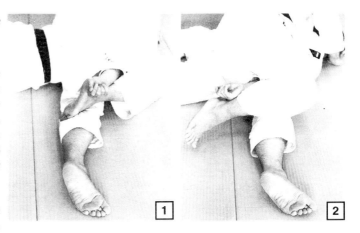

1) This picture shows the armlock attack of photograph 4 page 151 from above. The opponent's right arm is trapped by my right leg but I cannot apply the armlock on because of his flexibility.

2) First of all, I move my hips around clockwise.

3) Keeping his arm trapped, I extend my right leg.

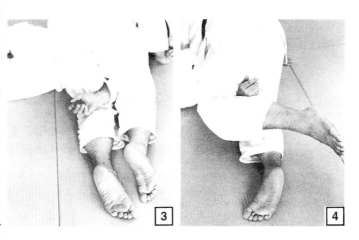

4-5) Next, I bend up my left leg and try the armlock from that side. In other words, by rearranging the position of the arm, I put the armlock on from the opposite direction.

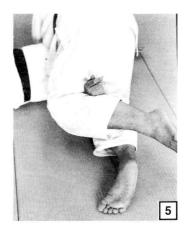

1) Attacking an opponent on all fours with *ashi-gatame*. This is the same method of attack as that shown in photograph 3 on page 150.

2) Your opponent tries to escape by putting his head in towards his trapped arm and turning his body. Using that movement, your right hand goes over his shoulder.

3-4) Move all your weight over towards his head. Your opponent will not be able to move from the position shown in photograph 3.

5) Hold him down with (*kuzure*) *kami-shiho-gatame*.

154

• Key points

Against an opponent who is defending on all-fours. How to disrupt his defence.

1) First pull him forward, grasping the back of his collar and his belt.
2) If you do this, he will put both arms forward in order to maintain his balance.
3) Take this opportunity and immediately take up his right arm with your right leg.

155

Ashi-gatame

1) With your opponent on all-fours, attack with *okuri-eri jime* from under his left arm.

2) In this case your opponent's method of counter-attack will probably be to clamp his left arm to his side (trapping your left hand) roll and hold down with *ushiro-kesa-gatame*. But, using your opponent's movement, you intentionally roll with him as if you were rolled up.

---

* Key Points

1) Against an opponent on all-fours, when you try to take his right arm to get into position for *ashi-gatame*, your opponent will defend by linking his arms.

2) If he gets into a defensive position with his arms linked together, his opposite armpit will loosen up and leave a gap. Immediately push your left hand into the gap and grab his left collar. He knows that if he lets go with his right hand, you will be able to apply the *ashi-gatame*, so he can't let go.

3) It is easy to get his left lapel with your left hand, and by pushing your left hand in and taking his collar, the *okuri-eri-jime* is a foregone conclusion.

3-4) Before your opponent can get into position for *ushiro-kesa-gatame*, push his right elbow with your right hand. Take care that your right hand does not get caught up, as he will then be able to hold you down.

5) As soon as you push his arm down, hook it with your left leg.

6) Secure the instep of your left foot behind your right knee and apply the armlock. With your right hand, take your opponent's left lapel and apply *okuri-eri-jime*.

Ryote-jime

(A) Against an opponent on all-fours.

1) With your opponent on all fours, from in front of him grip the back of his collar with the fingers inside the jacket, and push his head down. If you do this, he will raise his head to try and maintain his position.
2) Using his reaction of lifting his head up, pull his upper body up. At this point you can get plenty of slack between his collar and his neck. Therefore, in many cases, even if you take the lapel with your left hand your opponent will not be worried.
3) Take hold of the side lapel with your left hand fingers outside and opening your elbow....
4) Drop to your right knee, and pulling his upper body, quickly hook the right side of his jaw with your left wrist.
5-7) Pull both arms and hands in towards you, and as you push your weight onto him, strangle. There are quite a few cases in which the defender does not know how he has been strangled. It gives a feeling of being caught in a loop. If at stage 6, your opponent tries to escape by turning out, keep your weight on him and hold him down with *kuzure-kesa-gatame*.

(B) Against an opponent in a standing position.

1] Your opponent bends forward in a defensive posture. 2] Take both his lapels and pull downwards.
1-2) From a standing position, your opponent takes up a defensive, bent over posture. Pull down on both his lapels and lower his head. (In order to maintain the stability of his position, he will try to raise his head).
3) When you ease off on the downward pressure, his head will come up.
4) At that point, move slightly to the right.
5) With your left wrist, hook his right jaw around. (see side-view of the same position).
6-7) Pull in both elbows, close up your armpits, upset his balance and knock him down. Strangle from that position.

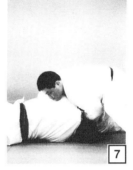

Time and again in practice, there were occasions when my opponent, having tried an attack, fell into a position on all-fours. With this repetitive behaviour, I couldn't get on with the practice and I couldn't attempt *ippon* scoring techniques. So, having thought about how to attack an opponent in this position, I came up with *ryote-jime*. When I started an attack with this technique, the opponent used to get the feeling that this position was rather dangerous and eventually would not take it up again. Consequently, standing work became much easier for me. In my first All-Japan Tournament against Nakagawa, this method proved very helpful.

159

Ude-gatame

Catching the arm from a standing position

1) In a *kenka-yotsu* grip, your *hikite* contends with that of your opponent for the advantage. Your opponent is gripping on the inside with his right hand, giving a sensation of bracing against you.

2) I put my left elbow in over my opponent's right arm from the outside.

3) Turning the wrist, I rotate the arm and link hands with my right hand around the area of his right elbow.

4) When you pull in towards your stomach, the armlock goes on. However in many cases, your opponent will try to escape the pressure by twisting forwards.

5-6) Catch your opponent between your legs as he is turning and completely stop his movement.

7) Hold him down.

There were many cases when my opponent used a right-handed grip - which meant a *kenka-yotsu* grip for me - and defended in a right stance, bracing on the inside with his *tsurite*, while not letting me take hold of his *hikite*.
I used this *ude-gatame* as a counter-measure against this type of player.

Contest tips 7 : Combining techniques

My best throws are *osoto-gari*, *uchimata* and *ouchi-gari*, but there is nothing much to be proud of in the power of individual throws. The one thing I can declare with confidence is that my throwing to groundwork combinations are quite good. The most important point in the connection between standing and ground techniques is that you must totally control your opponent's movement right up to the point you start your groundwork, and that, having thrown him, even at times when you think it must be an *ippon*, don't relax, but think of your next move. The person who will decide if it was an *ippon* or not is the referee. Never make your own judgement. In other words, you could say that the key to connecting your techniques is anticipating your opponent's move and getting there before him. Your opponent, who has just been thrown, is thinking solely of defence and there is no room in his head for thinking about his next move. It is here that your advantage in throwing him lies. If the contest is very evenly matched, there are very few winning chances let alone chances of throwing with *ippon*. Therefore, combinations are a great weapon to open up the way to victory. The most often used strategy of my victories was this throw to groundwork pattern.

Ouchi-gari to a hold-down. (yoko-shiho-gatame or kesa-gatame etc.)

1-2. Attack with left *ouchi-gari*.

3-4. As you knock him down, think about positioning your body on the inner side of your opponent. As a general rule you should always relate your position and posture to those of your opponent.

5. Sinking your body downwards, step in to your opponent's body from the knee of your sweeping leg (left) and firmly finish off the technique (*ouchi-gari*). Keep your hold on his *gi* just as it is.

6. Having thrown him, immediately pull him in towards you and push your chest into him.

7. Hold him down securely. If your finishing is sloppy at stage 5, your opponent will turn out and escape the hold.

163

Combinations from standing to groundwork

• Key points when combining techniques.

1. Don't let go once you have thrown him. In that instant, if he is set free, he will escape.
2. Always control your opponent and keep your body in close contact with his.
3. When you move into a hold, take your time and finish it properly. If you try to do it quickly you will bungle it.

1-3). I throw with *tai-otoshi*. My opponent so as not to lose by *ippon*, tries to twist out.
4) Having finished the throw, I immediately pull my hands in towards my chest to maintain control over my opponent so he cannot turn out.
5) Controlling my opponent, I use my weight fully and take up a holding position.
6-8) Carefully, close your body down onto him and hold. (*yoko-shiho-gatame* or *kuzure-kami-shiho-gatame*.)

Katame-waza in competition–kuzure-kesa-gatame

April 1976 Against Hara in the All-Japan Tournament quarter finals.

This is a photograph from my first All-Japan Tournament when I was seventeen. I remember it well.

Relations with my opponent, Hara, were bad even in practice. I had no confidence of winning with groundwork. However, as my opponent tried a technique, so I blocked it and in no time at all it seemed, he was on all fours and I was attacking him. Maybe because of my weight, I was suddenly in a good situation.

Then using the methods Sato *sensei* had taught me, I pulled out his left sleeve with my right hand and held him down with *kuzure-kesa-gatame*.

Katame-waza in competition–yoko-shiho-gatame

October 1983. Against Willie Wilhelm of The Netherlands in the over 95 kg category final of the world championship.
I blocked my Wilhelm's attempted technique and attacked from behind him with *okuri-eri-jime*. He disliked this attack and turned out. As he tried to escape I firmly applied a *yoko-shiho-gatame*. My body was completely over his head so that in form it was almost *kuzure-kami-shiho-gatame*. Wilhelm, at 195 cm tall and 135 kg was very strong. If he had tried to reverse that hold using his rather superhuman strength by bridging and twisting, then hugging me to him and turning over, the boot would have been on the other foot.
So, in order to prevent this occurrence, I pushed hard into his chest with my chin. The left hand controlling between his legs was necessary to guard against him twisting out to the right. In the case of very large opponents, it is essential that you lower your centre of gravity and don't get on top of his body too much.

April 1980 Against Endo in the final of the All-Japan Championships

As Endo came in for a left *harai-goshi* (he is right-handed), he was vulnerable to the rear. At that moment I moved into groundwork and from *okuri-eri-jime* switched to *yoko-shiho-gatame* and held him down.

1) I put my right hand deep in, to hold his head and could tightly control his neck by turning my wrist .

2) My left leg is balanced on the toes so that it can respond immediately to my opponent's movements. My left knee is in his side so he cannot catch it and I put some weight onto it. The right leg is extended for reasons of balance.

Note that this leg is on its toes.

December 1979 Against Turin of the USSR in the over 95kg category at the world championship in Paris

Photo sequence

1) This photograph depicts the point at which, having feinted wiith an *osoto- gari*, I immediately attacked with *sasae-tsuri-komi-ashi* and tried to throw my opponent forwards. Guarding against the backward throw, Turin became completely unbalanced by the technique in the opposite direction. The pull of the *tsurite* (left hand) and the pushing up of the *hikite* (right hand) worked well. Also, the left leg is already preparing for the transition to groundwork.

2) I got *waza-ari* with this technique. It is important never to let go of your grip even after throwing your opponent. You must not be too hasty in going in for a hold-down. The most important point in connecting standing with groundwork is to completely control your opponent's body.

In this example, I didn't let go of Turin, my chest was stuck firmly to his and I confined his movements. The body's actions in the split second when you throw (or for your opponent are thrown) dictate the winning or losing of a contest. In the moments after this photograph, I held him down with *yoko-shiho-gatame*.

169

Ashi-gatame to kuzure-kami-shiho-gatame

November 1982 Against Turin of the USSR in the open-weight category of the Kano Cup.

In this photograph I have trapped my opponent's right arm and am going for the *ashi-gatame*. Turin is trying to get out of the technique by turning to the side. In response to this movement, still in the ashi-gatame position, I control his right shoulder firmly and move into *kuzure-kami-shiho-gatame*. At 203 cm tall and 145 Kg my opponent is huge and I can't afford to let him have freedom of movement in his arms and shoulders. The point is that when you apply *ashi-gatame* you should control the right shoulder and not allow your opponent to move. I scored *ippon* with this *kuzure-kami-shiho-gatame*.

September 1981 Against Reszko in the final of the open-weight category at the world championships in Maastricht.

I attacked with k*osoto-gari*, and Reszko fell onto all-fours, I attacked from behind and put on *okuri-eri-jime*.

The right hand is fairly shallow, but as I am pulling enough on the right lapel with my left hand, the technique can be completed. If this pull on the left hand had been insufficient, I don't think that this technique would have been successful.

Another point to note is that I was pressing down on him with my chest and thereby restricting his movements. Reszko tapped just after this photograph was taken.

Training

Training

My Physical Training

It is only recently that emphasis has been put on the necessity of physical training in judo. In the past there have been, of course, various methods practised in order to build up and reinforce one's physique, but well-planned systematic training using modern equipment such as barbells etc. is still fairly new

My own physical training as described in this chapter must therefore be regarded as very basic, particularly by specialists. However, I thought that my own experience might be of interest as embodying a necessary stage in the development of judo training and so I decided to introduce it here.

There are a number of well-known books on physical training programmes which are of a very high standard. I would like readers to improve their own training methods by using such manuals and to use my own personal experiences as an examples of such a programme

1) Lacking basic physical strength.

In 1973, when I was in the first year at high school (sixteen years old), I won the All-Japan High School Championship in the heavy-weight category. I was chosen to join the National Junior Squad Team. When I look back at my physical strength then, it was not so bad compared to other high school students but it was far from the standards of international competitors. This is illustrated by my physical statistics measured in December that year at the national squad training camp in Tokyo.

"He weighs too much for his height and has too much fat. His average score of 2.8 is the worst and he doesn't seem to be well trained at all. This score of 2.8 out of 10 in physical functions can be regarded as utterly pitiful."

Physical Statistics (Main Items)
Measured at the national squad training camp 21/12/1973

Figures

Height	179.0 cm
Head Size	45.4 cm
Chest size	117.5 cm
Upper arm	
Flexed	
Left	43.0 cm
Right	44.2 cm
Relaxed	
Left	41.0 cm
Right	41.8 cm
Thigh Right	67.8 cm
Left	69.5 cm
Calf Right	48.2 cm
Left	47.6 cm
Subcutaneous Fat (Stomach)	32.0 cm
Weight	121.6 Kg

Functions

Sidesteps per minute	38
Press-ups	40
H.S.T point per second	79.8
Vertical jump	48.0 cm
Gripping power	
Right	65.0 Kg
Left	56.0 Kg
Back Muscles	140.8 Kg
Pulling power	160.9 Kg
Forward flexibility	8.8 cm
Backward flexibility	46.0 cm
Body reaction per second	379.6 cm
Breathing capacity	5200 cc

I fully realised when I compared my result with the good results of all my senior colleagues that I had to give priority to physical training if I were to become number one in Japan and the world. Thinking about it, it was only natural that I should attain my goal, as before then I had only ever done randori or uchikomi in the dojo and had done no muscle training. As far as I remember, I had only ever done a few bench presses with 70 kg barbells and probably a few press-ups, let alone any running. It was far from a systematic and well-planned training programme. Joining the national squad camp, therefore taught me an enormous amount.

2) The physical strength needed for judo.

It is not always the case that the stronger you get the better a judo player you become. You have to realise that physical strength must be combined with judo techniques. Even if you can left very heavy barbells, it doesn't mean anything unless you can translate that power into your judo.

The following are my methods and definitions of physical strength in judo:

1) Building up strength through randori.
Especially with bigger and better partners, and without compromise, you can build on the overall strength of your body. In judo the curved line power is more effective than that of the straight line and it is important to master such power in your movements. However, there are some sorts of power which cannot be gained from judo practice alone.

2) Through physical training.
You should build up your overall strength as well as that specifically connected to your favourite techniques. As power (mus-cle strength x speed) is especially required in judo, it is essential to focus on muscle building and more importantly to apply the result of this training into randori. For example, in building up your muscles, it is not really necessary to "release all your power" but the key point of randori is how to "let loose your power momentarily and achieve a state of *kyo* (emptiness)". If you can't do this, you will probably be criticised: " You are so stiff because of all that muscle training".

3) Establish your own style by increasing your strength.

I would like to introduce my own training programme. The three main points of my attack and defence strategy were to:
a) Control the timing
b) Grip from underneath
c) Use my *hikite* efficiently.
In order to achieve these three points I undertook the regime which follows over the page.

For a) Bench press : 4 or 5 sets of weights between 100 and 140 Kg
                                100 Kg = 12 times per set
                                140 Kg = 4 or 5 times per set

For b) Dumbbell curls : (@ 30 kgs)

For c) Chest / Waist : Lifting heavy weights in a single movement (using the
                            chest and waist as well as the arms).

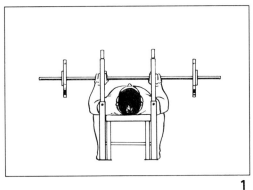

1   2

Bench Press

This is the most popular method of training. You should aim to be able to push up
the weight equivalent of your body-weight without difficulty.
1 Hold the barbell at your shoulders' width above your chest.
2 Push up straight

1   2

Dumbbell Curl

1 Hold a dumbbell in each hand
2 Lift one up to the shoulder
3 As one goes down, lift the other
    one up.

3   4

1

2

3

1

2

3

1

2

3

Pulley training

This exercise should be done with speed. It is useful for increasing power in the areas most important in judo i.e. *hiku* and *osu* (pull and push)

1   Lifting with one hand
2   Lifting with both hands. You should use a combination of your *hikite* and *tsurite*.
3   *Tsurite* training

As a result of the above, although my physical strength was not yet good enough, I started to control the timing in my contests from the time I won the National Championships (when I was twenty years old) onwards. To have good timing means not to be pulled towards the opponent from above (my weak point was being gripped from above and pulled in by an opponent of kenka-yotsu grip) and this training enabled me to build up my own style of judo. All this hard training started to have an effect on my body shape. I remember my jacket. In the autumn of my first year at university, I tried to wear a jacket which had been made for the overseas tour two years previously. I could not fit into the jacket because the sleeves were too tight. My weight and height did not change drastically but my body shape was very different.

4) Tackling your weak points

I hated running, probably because I was so fat. Running affects the respiration and circulation and is a good way of improving your stamina, but it is such a difficult job for fat people. It is, I suppose, human nature to want to avoid something painful. You must, however, try to tackle what you hate when it is obvious that you cannot overcome your weaknesses without it. Once you have decided to do it, it is important to have a positive mental attitude in order to get good results. No whining!

I made myself have a positive attitude and received appropriate advice from Sato *sensei*. I was always last in the running but never gave up. It is also vital to have this positive attitude to maintain physical

Sprinting on the track with my great friend, rival and team-mate Hitoshi Saito

strength. I was always aiming at improving my physical strength, not just maintaining it. But, as you get older, your physique starts to decline and your strength cannot continue to grow. In my case, my peak was as far as figures are concerned, the ages of twenty-four and twenty-five. There was no sign of improvement after that. On the other hand, in my mind, I was still trying to improve. I think this mental attitude helped a lot, at least to maintain the strength I had.

5) How to cope with physical degeneration.

I started to get injured more easily as I got older, and the fatigue was building up. In contrast to my eagerness, my body stamina was decreasing. In Moscow, when I tore a shoulder muscle, Sato *sensei* said to me, *"The full moon has passed. We shall concentrate on strength training and alter our methods."*

I then planned the following programme according to Sato *sensei's* advice.

1) When I think there isn't enough time devoted to strength training in a practice I finish judo early and do the weight training instead.

2) I had mainly been doing weights and running but I tried other methods to stimulate my body from a different approach. Sometimes I played tennis or rode a bicycle. It was very successful and had a good effect not only on physical strength but on the spiritual side. It was good for changing my mood. From the age of 27, I tried shot putting, hammer throwing and javelin. I sometimes joined in the physical training of the athletics club and I learned a lot from their well-planned sessions.

3) I directed a lot of my attention towards not tiring myself out. I combined nutrition and resting (you still build up strength even when you are resting) with my training plan. As a result I had a lot less to drink. This moderation in drinking could probably be said to be the best effect of all my training.

Working out with weights to develop the strength in the shoulders that is so vital for judo.

6. Training to overcome injuries.

No matter how much care you take, you can still get injured. I had the experience of breaking my left fibula when I was 23 and suffering a torn right calf muscle at 27. The methods of recovery training differ case by case depending on the person and the region of the injury. In my case, I paid attention to the following points:

1) Do not repeat the injury i.e. do not make the same mistake twice.
2) Complete your recovery as quickly as possible by paying close attention to medical advice and being careful not to cause a recurrence of the injury.
3) Limit the reduction in your physical strength as much as possible in both the injured part and in all other parts of your body.
4) Never be too hasty. Don't let your impatience get the better of you.

Looking back at the time when I broke my fibula, my recovery training was as follows:

1] Hospital Treatment (about 2 months)
Rehabilitation of the damaged area. Plus some isometric training with the plaster cast still on (static training). Through this I guarded against the weakening of the physical strength in my calf. For upper body and right leg training I used dumb bells and sand bags in the rehabilitation room and in bed. About one hour each in the morning and afternoon.

2] Immediately after hospital treatment
I still wasn't able to run yet. Fighting my impatience, and being careful not to harm the injury, I gradually took on more each day as the situation improved. If I felt in the least bit strange, I stopped training. When I returned to a normal condition, I would look at the situation again and restart my training. I also did weight-training and swimming. The swimming was very effective in the recovery of my respiratory and circulatory functions.

3] 2 months after treatment.
I started to run slowly.

4] 3 months after.
Judo practice resumed, starting with *uchikomi*.

5] 4 months after.
I took part in the All-Japan squad camp and managed to better my personal record in weight training with bench presses and squats.

6] About 6 months after.
Randori. I resumed my original condition.

7] 9 months after.
I entered a competition –The All-Japan Tournament

In my case, after I resumed training there was no relapse with my injury. In this year, it was very fortuitous that there were no big events like international tournaments staring me in the face, so I could pay proper attention to medical treatment and recovery training.

After being injured with a torn calf muscle in the Los Angeles Olympics, because every day was pressurised, I couldn't do enough recovery training and my recovery was fairly slow.

In any case, no matter how strong you are, injuries are always a bind. I can say from my own experience that having an injury on your hands while leading the life of a judo player is a great burden. You have to bear in mind that if you are injured you become just another player. (See Chapter 1 " On winning and losing" page 22).

7. How far should you push yourself ?

If you are injured in a competition should you continue to compete? Or, if you are injured before a competition, should you enter or not?

For these questions, everyone's "objective" becomes the key point to the decision. In principle, you should stop at the point the injury happens as it is best to avoid forcing the injury and making it worse. However, if you believe that the competition is the most important for you as a player - in other words if you feel that

"I'm going to give everything in this contest, even if recovery is difficult afterwards" – you had better continue in spite of the damage it will cause. Of course, this is how I felt at the Los Angeles Olympics.

In the end, the basis of judgement is each person's objective. Your coach and the surrounding people are shouting " Go on!" and if you say you are going to stop, they may shout " You've got no balls!" but an injury is the injured person's problem and in the aftermath he is the one who will bear the effects of the injury. Therefore, you should always make adequate preparations for eventualities such as these.

The meaning of training

The word "training" has recently become familiar to the Japanese as an adopted foreign word. If this word "training" is translated into Japanese it is *'kunren'*-training; *'renshu'*-practice; and *'tanren'*-discipline/skill according to the dictionary. In daily life, we often say "train your body" and "train your mind" and if we put these sayings into the context of sport they are covered by the foreign word "training".

People have all different sorts of abilities. In sports muscle power is one of those abilities. In order to build up and develop your strength, you must train at the right time by the right method. You could say that if we relate this to training, the well-known saying "strike while the iron is hot" very simply expresses the importance of good timing and effective methods. In the arts of judo and kendo, it is customary to call this process of discipline *"keiko"*, loosely translated as study or discipline. It is justifiable to think that in general, the meaning is synonymous with that of "training". In Japan there is a general tendency to call any practice done in the *dojo* centred around *randori* "keiko" and all other practice to build up the body such as running, dumb bells etc. "training". Accordingly, when we say "training" we usually mean body training.

It is very important to have an aim in your training. Even if it is a futile aspiration, as long as you have the dream you can at least get on the path you want to follow. For each person the aim is different but if you have an objective you can set up a concrete programme directed towards that aim. Your training programme should be such that it shows the way to climb to the peak of your ambition and having climbed slowly but surely up the ladder it will enable you to attain your goal.

There is a great difference between long and short term programmes. "Short term" can mean a year, a month, or maybe just a week. In addition, the programme could be group-based e.g. society, club etc. or individually-based.

In junior and senior high school and university the programme is based on the ideas of the teacher, but while performing the practice on that basis it is important that you establish personal goals for your own progress. This is because there is a great difference in progress according to attitudes among those who practice following the groups' aims. There are those who do what they are told and those who practice with a sense of their personal goals. If you have a constructive attitude you will come to see your problem areas for yourself. When you become a university student and begin to seriously consider your independence, it will be difficult to progress if you don not have this sort of positivity.

Judo does not consist of just one person. It is important that you have a good teacher and good training partners and in that vein you should cultivate co-operative relationships with as many people as possible. When drawing up your training programme it is important not to forget this and to take care not to design it arbitrarily.

As an example of a training programme, I set out below Tokai University's training programme for 1990. Especially as a teacher's reference.

1) Approximately 100 students are divided into four groups by weight.

Light-weight   (-60 and -65)
 4 groups
Middle-weight   (-71 and -78)

Light heavy-weight   (-86 and -95)

Heavy-weight   (over 95)

2) Divide up the training period and vary the content.

a Period of many competitions –
April to beginning of November
    (Season)
b Few competitions –
Mid-November to March
    (Off-season)

3) Conduct the normal strength tests.

4) Each person has training notes so they can compare with their past records. At the same time, in the weight training area we stick up a record paper.

5) Training contents
a) During the season
Morning: 40 mins from 7 o'clock: running or weights

                    (4 times a week)
 Afternoon: About 3 hours judo
                    (6 times a week)
An example of morning training for the light-weight group....
Running: 1) 4-5 Kms (@25 mins) roadwork

           2) Dash   (30m x 10)
           3) Piggyback (30m x 2)
           4) Fireman's lift (30m x 2)
           5) Push ups (50 x 3 sets)

Weight training: 1) Bench Press
2) Squats
3) Abdominals
4) Curls
5) Chest

b) Off-season Physical renewal and overcoming inertia.

In the morning training we sometimes include ball sports with lots of movement such as basketball or soccer. In the weight-training we try for increase in body strength and power build up. In the afternoon too, we don't just do judo but include other fighting sports such as sambo or wrestling and increase the weight-training and running.

Strength and exercise

"Strength" is a vague concept which has a wide variety of meanings. When implementing your training you should address the idea of "necessary strength".

This concept is often clarified by dividing strength into the "physical element" and "spiritual element". These two elements are made up of defensive strength (resistance to external forces) and aggressive strength (forcing an impression on the outside world). Using these divisions, if we think about strength from the standpoint of exercise, physical strength comes to the fore. To develop defensive strength, you need intense practice and training in order to push yourself to the limit, at places such as toughening up practice and summer training camps. This is because with this sort of stimulation, body exhaustion is extreme, the strain on your mind and body reaches a peak and your resistance to illness is weakened.

Exercise is conducted through general biological functions such as muscle contraction and relaxation, breathing to supply energy, and the workings of the circulatory system in regulation of the brain and nervous system. Thus in training it is important to recognise these functions and the effects of training on them. The important points of training from the point of view of human biological functions are the following:

1) When you train you see an improvement in the efficiency of these functions

2) When you cease training, efficiency will decline.

Moderation is essential as "over-use" and "dis-use" are always detrimental factors in training.

There are various ways of training your body e.g. weight-training, isometric training, interval training etc. In this chapter I am limiting myself to recounting my personal experiences and have curtailed accounts of methods and explanations of training exercises such as these. When you put them into practice, refer to a specialist book, listen carefully to your teachers' instructions and always do the exercises in the correct manner.

Principles of exercise

Before and after training.
You should warm up and cool down properly. Especially with cooling down you often see people who finish off very simply, but it is necessary to cool down fully until your body is completely relaxed.

1. Overload
Exceeding the exercise load over and above a fixed level. Exercise below this level is easy. Lazy talk such as "I want to take it easy and enjoy myself" is not on. When exercising you should carefully consider the intensity of your training, how long you spend, and the frequency.

2. Individuality
Biological faculties differ from person to person. You should select the method which suits you best. My own method would not really be appropriate for everyone.

3. Gradual Progression
You should increase the relative difficulty of your exercise (intensity and load) little by little. Suddenly undertaking extreme exercise is a common cause of injuries. Cramming is not a good idea.

4. Continuity
Exercise is effective if conducted continuously over a long period. A hard and steady worker will accomplish a lot more than an unsteady one. A strong player is one who climbs step by step. A weak one will fall down the hill.

5. Comprehensiveness
You should exercise so as to develop your whole body in balance. With food too, an unbalanced diet can become a cause of illness. You should think of your body as a whole and use the large range of exercises available.

6. Self-reliance/ Subjectivity
Know the purpose of your exercise and appreciate the effect of it. It is not somebody making you do something but is more a matter of following it up by yourself. In training, it is important to consider a balance between exercise, nutrition and relaxation and base your principles of exercise on these factors.

184

Training in Europe – results of a survey

After I retired from competition, I went to study in the UK for one year from August 1986 onwards. Taking this opportunity, I investigated the judo in various countries such as France, West Germany (Split from East Germany at that time), Switzerland and of course the UK. On my return to Japan, I presented the results of my survey to the Martial Arts Institute and Tokai University (Physical Educaton Dept.). I have set out below an outline of the section of that presentation concerned with training.

* Number of people involved in the survey: 469. 389 Men; 80 Women

   Of these 105 were International Players (IP).

* Average age 28.9 years (SD 11.23)

1) Practice place

An overwhelming 92.3% of the total and 90.5% of the IP replied "Club". In Japan there is a far greater percentage of those doing judo as a school PE subject.

2) Amount of Practice

   a) No. of practices per week (days)

      Total   2 X (29.2%) 3 X (24.5%) 4 X (14.7%)
      IPs   5 X (26.7%) 4X (21.0%)   7 X (18.1%)

      About 80% (79.1%) of International Players practice more than 4 times a week.

   b) Hours per practice

      For all players a range of 90 - 120 minutes was the general rule with the average for all players being 101 minutes.

3) Weight-training

      Total   2 X (15.1%)   3 X (11.9%)
      IPs   3 X (27.6%)   2 X (23.0%)

   The average time spent on each occasion was 68 minutes for all players and 73 minutes for IPs.

4) Running/Training (per week)

      Total   2 X (19.2%)   1 X (18.1%)
      IPs   2 X (23.8%)   3 X (22.9%)

   The average time spent on each occasion was 44.3 minutes for all players and 46.6 minutes for IPs.

5) Others.

      About 30% of all players and 60% of IPs trained to improve their competitiveness through other sports such as cycling, basketball, tennis, canoing, skiing, soccer etc.

The players who were the subject of this survey all have excellent competitiveness. If we compare them with Japan, the amount of judo they do is less than that of Japanese players but there is more physical training. In Europe, where there is not a great abundance of practice partners, the idea that there is a direct connection betwen development of body strength and increase in competitiveness seems to be prevalent. The figures seem to back up the saying "Japan for technique: Europe for strength".

In this book, I have introduced my speciality techniques but they are only a part of the large number of judo techniques available. They have been put together from my own experiences and on the basis of my physical characteristics and personality. All readers, especially those just starting judo should recognise this point and pick out the basic and practical parts of my technical expanation. This book should be used as one of many references.

As I have compiled this book around contest and technique, I have not included chapters especially devoted to fundamental judo such as posture, gripping, breaking balance, body control and ukemi; referee regulations, rules or history. Accordingly, you should learn about these judo basics from other sources. Not only in judo, but in whatever you are doing, you cannot expect to accomplish anything if you neglect the basics. For example we have the saying "start with *ukemi*, finish with *ukemi*". The beauty and power of techniques are the result of long years of effort.

Elementary knowledge

1) Judo techniques - page 188
2) Parts of the judo gi - page 187
3) Judo kata
As methods of practicing judo techniques we have *randori* and *kata*. *Kata* is a form of practice which sets out the order of attack and defence in advance, whereas *randori* involves mutually independent attack and defence. Recently, the trend has been not to practice much *kata*. I myself am not very good at it but kata is very good for the learning of judo theory and a wide range of techniques.

Various sorts of kata.
1) *Nage-no-kata* (kata of throws) 15 variations
2) *Katame-no-kata* (kata of groundwork) 15 variations (Randori kata)
3) *Kime-no-kata* (kata of decisive techniques) 20 variations
4) *Ju-no-kata* (kata of non-resistance) 15 variations
5) *Koshiki-no-kata* (antique style kata) 21 variations
6) *Itsutsu-no-kata* (kata of five movements. Imitating water) 5 variations
7) *Goshin-jitsu-no-kata* (Kodokan Art of Self-defence) 21 variations
8) *Seiryoku zenyo kokumin taiiku no kata* (kata of people's physical education with the principle of best use of mind and body)

4) Competition rules
Competitions are conducted under well-established rules. Nowadays there are two sets of rules: the Kodokan Judo Competition Rules and the International Judo Federation (IJF) rules. Which is used depends on the competition. International competitions always use the IJF rules. For the rule details you should read the rule book carefully as it is important to have a good graps of all regulations. Be sure that you are reading the most recently revised version.

5) Basic Movements
1] *Posture*
Standing • Natural position *shizentai* (standing naturally with equal tension throughout the body). Left natural, natural, right natural.
  • Defensive position *jigotai* (feet further apart than in the natural position, both knees are bent and the body is lowered.

2] *How to fight*

Standing / Groundwork

3] *Gripping*

• How to grip from a natural position
• How to grip from a defensive position

4] *Advancing / retreating movement*

Moving forwards, backwards, left or right as the situation demands.
How to walk in judo:
• *Ayumi-ashi* (stepping with alternate feet)
• *Tsugi-ashi* (one foot leads the other follows).

5] *Breaking balance*

In order to easily apply your techniques, you have to force your opponent into an unstable position. This is the most important principle of judo. There are eight basic directions in which you can unbalance your opponent.

6] *Body control*

This is the ability to move into the most suitable position, whether in attack or defence, while keeping your poise and balance.
• Forward
• Backward
• Forward turning
• Backward turning

7 *Setting up and applying judo principles*

• Unbalance your opponent (setting up your opponent
• Manoeuvre yourself to the best position. Posture and balance to use your technique.(setting yourself up).
• Applying – carrying out the technique you just set up.

8] *Ukemi*

The method of minimising damage to your body and falling safely when thrown by your opponent or by yourself.

JUDO TECHNIQUES

THROWING

HAND	HIP	LEG	SACRIFICE	SIDE SACRIFICE
Seoi-nage	Uki-goshi	De-ashi-barai	Tomoe-nage	Yoko-otoshi
Tai-otoshi	O-goshi	Hiza-guruma	Sumi-gaeshi	Tani-otoshi
Kata-guruma	Koshi-guruma	Sasae-tsuri komi-ashi	Ura-nage	Hane-maki-komi
Sukui-nage	Tsuri-komi goshi	Osoto-gari	Hiki-komi-gaeshi	Soto-maki-komi
Uki-otoshi	Harai-goshi	Ouchi-gari	Tawara-gaeshi	Uki-nage
Sumi-otoshi	Tsuri-goshi	Kosoto-gari		Yoko-wakare
Obi-otoshi	Hane-goshi	Kouchi-gari		Yoko-guruma
Seoi-otoshi	Utsuri-goshi	Okuri-ashi-barai		Yoko-kakari (gake)
Yama-arashi	Ushiro-goshi	Uchimata		Daki-wakare
Sode-gari		Kosoto-gake		Uchi-maki-komi
Kuchiki-taoshi		Ashi-guruma		Kani-basami
Kibisu-gaeshi		Harai-tsuri-komi-ashi		Kashin-gake
Uchimata-sukashi		Oguruma		Osoto-maki-komi
Kouchi-gaeshi		Osoto-guruma		Uchimata-maki-komi
		Osoto-otoshi		Harai-maki-komi
		Tsubame-gaeshi		
		Osoto-gaeshi		
		Ouchi-gaeshi		
		Hane-goshi-gaeshi		
		Harai-goshi-gaeshi		
		Uchi-mata-gaeshi		

GROUNDWORK

HOLDS	STRANGLES	ARMLOCKS
Hon-kesa-gatame	Nami-juji-jime	Ude-gatame
Kuzure-kesa-gatame	Gyaku-juji-jime	Hiza-gatame
Kata-gatame	Kata-juji-jime	Waki-gatame
Kami-shiho-gatame	Hadaka-juji-jime	Hara-gatame
Kuzure-kami-shiho	Okuri-eri-jime	Ashi-gatame
Yoko-shiho-gatame	Kata-ha-jime	Te-gatame
Tate-shiho-gatame	Kata-te-jime	Sangaku- gatame
	Ryote-jime	
	Sode-guruma	
	Tsuki-komi-jime	
	Sangaku-jime	

Postcript by Nobuyuki Sato

Yasuhiro Yamashita

Our Relationship
as Player and Coach

Nobuyuki Sato and Yasuhiro Yamashita watching a competition.

Introduction

It was November 1984 and we were attending the Austrian Open in Vienna when Yamashita said to me "*Sensei*, I'm going to retire". I was shocked by this sudden announcement and hoped that he would still continue. As I listened to him, however, I realised that he was far more physically and mentally exhausted than I had realised. We had never had anyone in our judo history like Yamashita who had achieved as much as he did and had such a wealth of experience. In a word, Yamashita was a "superhero". I realised that no-one could understand the feelings of someone who achieved something for the first time in history.

In the summer when Yamashita came to Tokyo from Kumamoto with a great ambition to become the champion of Japan and the world, our three-legged race began. Since that time I have been his coach but it has been me who has learned from him. That is to say I became a better person because I met someone whose ability was much greater than mine, and therefore my ability as a coach improved. I thank him for this.

There were many people who supported him from the time he was a "*kaido*" (gifted child) until he grew up and became "*kaibutsu*" (superhero). Mr Shigeyoshi Matsumae, the President of Tokai University provided us with a suitable setting in which we could devote ourselves to judo practice. The environment is the most important factor when bringing up sports players. I also thank Mr Isao Inokuma the manager, and many other staff from the Tokai judo club.

I am pleased to have been given the opportunity to write a section for this book, the first technical book on judo by Yasuhiro Yamashita. I hope it will help readers to understand this great player. It is adapted from an article I wrote for the magazine of the International Olympic Committee.

The relationship between player and coach.

There are many different angles from which to discuss the relationship between player and coach. One of them is to look at it from the coach's point of view when the two players first meet. It is the best feeling you can ever have as a coach when you find a player in whom you can see a great potential. I had exactly this feeling when I first met Yamashita. To coach him meant to challenge my own ability as a coach.

It is not easy to become number one in the world. There are so many players who are aiming for the gold medal in the Olympic Games or the world championships but there are only a few who can actually make it. The coach and player have the single aim of becoming number one.

A player with potential will be just an ordinary person if he doesn't fulfil his potential. This is the point of a well-known Japanese proverb: " From ordinary stone to a work of art". In order to get a gold medal, good conditions and good teaching methods are essential. Those conditions and methods vary from player to player and from country to country but there are many similarities.

There are three conditions that are always necessary to coach gold medallists - applicable to any sport, not just judo. They are:

1) The player must have three essential elements, namely "*shin*" (mental strength); "*gi*" (technique); and "*tai*" (physical power).

2) Appropriate training in both quality and quantity.

3) A good environment for practice.

Here, the environment means coach, partners, family, school work place, and national support. Yamashita is a successful example who satisfied all the above three conditions.

My advice for Yamashita on his loss of fighting spirit.

Despite all his advantages, Yamashita did have problems. In 1982, the year after he had won two categories in the world championships and his sixth consecutive title in the Japan championship, he told me "*Sensei*, I seem to have lost my fighting spirit. Why?" Yamashita claimed that he didn't have the energy to fight, even against Hitoshi Saito, his greatest rival. I told him to think it over by himself and then a month later I asked him if he'd found the reason. He answered, " I think because I'm too busy writing my thesis for my finals and have no time for judo". I scolded him. "Who do you think you are?" I said. His face fell and he assumed the serious expression he wears in tournaments. "What do you mean? I had a reason." When I recommended that he should practise *uki-waza* he refused to practise it even before trying , giving excuses such as "I have a stiff back". I told him " Yamashita, you may be a better player than I am , so I can only guess at how you feel, but I recommend this technique because I believe you will need it. Yet, you refuse even before trying it. You are being very selfish. You can't even win against Saito by *ippon* can you?"

He couldn't help showing anger, but in a short while he started to practise this technique without another word. It goes without saying that he mastered the technique. The players who win a major tournament should naturally have enough talent to win again, but there are not that many players who can actually win continuously.

This question of how to maintain the player's motivation is the biggest issue for the coaches.

I set out the following agenda to overcome this problem.

1) Provide stable environmental conditions for practice. In Japan, it is important to maintain the environment especially in the first few years after graduation from university and we should work on this issue in Japan immediately.

2) Establish a scholarship system

3) Teach players the value of making records and challenging them.

4) Teach players that physical strength is limited but there is no limit to technique. Before reaching the top players always have a desire to become number one. In order to maintain this spirit, it is necessary to set a new goal each time they achieve something and to extend their technique and maintain good practice conditions. In the case of Yamashita his motivation was maintained by points 1, 3 and 4.

Setting goals

The most important task of the coach is to set goals. In general there are some basic training rules;

1) To give better students harder training than average.
2) To gradually increase the difficulty and hardness of training.

3) To continue training for an extended term.

4) To let players understand the purpose and the effects of training so that
    they can practise confidently

5) To find a suitable method for each player and not just concentrate on a
    single method.

In the case of Yamashita, ever since he was small he had dreamed of becoming the Olympic champion. His aims under Mr Shiraishi in junior high school were to become a champion in the High School Championship in his first year and to win the All-Japan championship in his third year. As far as the Olympic Games were concerned, Moscow was boycotted but he coveted the gold in the Los Angeles Olympics. The result was, as we all know, that he won despite injury. It is sad, then, to learn that even a player like Yamashita has to face times when he cannot motivate himself.

I always try to set two different types of goals. One is the final, larger goal and the other the easier, short term goal. For example, to win the Olympic Games would be the long-term goal and the short-term would be to win domestic tournaments. We have to approach short-term goals one by one and effectively. That is to say, we have to take account of various conditions and increase the goals gradually. There is no progress without goals. They are the main core of a player's motivation.

To have ears to listen

From my experience as a coach, I have concluded that the successful players are the obedient ones. It is human nature to become arrogant when one becomes famous, but I would give up players who start to show off. In ancient Japanese literature there is a saying "People with huge egos do not last long". This applies perfectly to the sports world. That is why coaching is so vital. Those players who listen to what their coaches say and practise without complaining can in the end achieve great honour. I call this spirit "to have ears to listen" When Yamashita came to Tokyo in his second year at high school, I warned him straight away. "If you become arrogant I will break your nose OK?" I was worried about the media treating him like a genius at that time and there has been virtually no-one who has succeeded after such treatment. The greatest part of Yamashita's character is that he has always been willing to listen even after he became a champion and even now when he is retired.

In the world of sport, one can be the top person when one is young. That is probably because of physical strength but it doesn't last long. The life after winning championships is much longer. A player who has won championships tends to have the illusion that he or she has conquered the world. The fact that they have made it can bring about a negative reaction which lasts for the rest of their lives. Honours in sport is just one of many honours achievable. This is something players must be taught. While coaching and aiming at the long-term goals we have to teach players how to apply what they have learned from sports to the rest of their life. Sports do not exist to create a winning machine. I didn't want Yamashita to become just a machine in order to win or to be a robot player who only moved as I ordered. I always wanted him to be someone who thinks, decides and fights by himself. He certainly showed me that aspect of himself in the All-Japan championships in 1985. I was very happy.

To teach is to learn

It has been said that in order to become an international player one-to-one coaching is best. This is not enough. Training needs to be related to medical science. The progress in scientific research in the sports world is remarkable. It is the generation of researching "*shin*", "*gi*" and "*tai*" scientifically. The coaches therefore need more passion, logic and technique than ever before, plus an ability to listen to players' problems and questions. We can gain trust from players in return for giving them advice. Coaches must study and research and have enough experience to back them up. As I mentioned at the beginning , to coach Yamashita was a great experience for me. There is a saying that teaching is learning. I can only wish that Yamashita continues to develop and grow as an individual by learning more and more in his career as a teacher.

Three generations of judo champions.
Nobuyuki Sato, Yasuhiro Yamashita, and Isao Inokuma (left to right).

The Victory Trail

Yr/Mth		Competition and level	Score	results	Remarks
1970	8	North Kyushu JHS tournament	2F 2W	Toen JHS win	
	11	Kumamoto ken JHS newcomers	3F 3W	Toen JHS win	
1971	7	" city JHS competition	4F 4W	Toen JHS win	
		" Individual 1st& 2nd yrs.	3F 3W	W	
	8	Kumamoto ken JHS competition	4F 4W	Toen JHS win	
		" Individual 1sr& 2nd yrs.	4F 4W	W	
	8	North Kyushu JHS Tournament	4F 4W	Toen JHS win	
	8	Kyushu JHS championships	4F 4W	Toen JHS win	
	8	All Japan JHS championships	6F 6W	Toen JHS win	
				2nd consecutive win	Ippon in all fights
1972	7	Kumamoto city JHS competition	4F 4W	Toen JHS win	
		" individual competition	4F 4W	W	
	8	" city JHS competition	4F 4W	Toen JHS win	
		" individual competition	5F 5W	W	
	8	North Kyushu JHS Tournament	4F 4W	Toen JHS win	
		" individual competition	5F 5W	W	
	8	Kyushu JHS championship	4F 4W	Toen JHS win	
		ken qualifier for national c'ships	5F 5W	Toen JHS win	
	8	All Japan JHS championships	5F 5W	Toen JHS win	
				3rd consecutive win	Ippon in all fights
1973	6	Interhigh ken qualifying round	6f 4W 2D	KGHS #2	
		" individual heavyweight	6F 6W	W	
	6	Kumamoto ken select competition	3F 3W	KGHS #2	
	6	Kyushu High School tournament	5F 5W	KGHS W	
	7	Kinshuki tournament	12F 11W 1L	KGHS #3	Lost on decision to Yoshioka
	8	Interhigh Individual heavyweight	7F 6W 1D	W	
	8	Kyushu qualifier for Nat.HS tournament	6F 6W		
	8	Kyusu HS Indvidual tournament	4F 4W	W	1st time a 1st yr. HS student wins
1974	2	Kumamoto Ken High School newcomers' tournament	4F 4W	KGHS W	
				KGHS #3	
	6	Interhigh Ken qualifying round	3F 3W	W	
		Interhigh Individual heavyweight	6F 6W	KGHS W	
	6	Kumamoto Ken select competition	5F 5W	KGHS W	
	7	Golden eagle banner tournament	10F 10W		
	8	Interhigh Individual heavyweight	4F 3W 1L	#3	Lost on decision to Matsui
	9	Tokai University Europe tour	13F 13W		
	11	Friendly competition vs. Germany	4F 4W		
1975	3	National squad Kanagawa ken qualifier	2F 1W 1D		Lost to Karui with Uchimata
	3	National squad Kanto area qualifier	6F 5W 1L	Picked for Nat sqad	Lost to Uemura
	4	All Japan tournament	4F 3W 1L	#3	(decision)
	5	Ken qualifier for Kanto area HS T'ment	2F 2W		
	5	Kanto Area High School Tournament	5F 5W	TU Sagami HS won	
	5	1st. qualifier for World championships	5F 3W 2L		Lost to Endo (d) &Ninomiya (10)
	7	2nd qualifier for World championships	1F 1L		Lost to Anzai (d)
	7	Interhigh ken qualifying round	6F 6W	Sagami won	
	7	Interhigh Individual heavyweight	6F 6W	W	
	7	Kinshuki tournament	11F 11W	Sagami won	

1975	8	Interhigh Team competitiion	8F 8W		
		" individual heavyweight	6F 6W	2nd in 2 years	
	9	Japan select tournament (heavy)	1F 1L		Lost to Endo (d)
	10	national High School tournament	8F 7W 1D	Kanagawa ken won	
	10	National newcomers qualifiers' category (heavy)	3F 3W	W	
	11	National newcomers category (heavy)	4F 4W	W	
1976	1	French Open heavyweight	5F 5W	W	
	2	First qualifier for Olympic Games	3F 3L		Lost to Uemura, Takagi & Ninomiya
	3	National championships Kanto Area qualifiers	4F 4W	selected	Lost to Endo & Uemura (d)
	4	2nd qualifier for Olympic Games	2F 2L		Lost to Uemura (d)
	4	National championships	3F 2W 1L		Lost to Endo (d)
	5	Tokyo student championships	5F 5W	Tokai U won	
	5	National Select Categorised tournament Heavywt.	2F 1W 1L		
	6	National Student Championships	4F 4W	Tokai U #2	
	10	National Students kanto kansai Tourna-ment	2F 1W 1D		
		" individual	5F 5W	W	1st first yr. ever
	11	National select team champions	6F 5W 1D	Tokai U #2	
	11	Tokyo Student newcomers	1F 1W		
	11	National newcomers Categories Tokyo qualifiers +93kg	4F 4W	W	
	11	National newcomers Categories +93kg	4F 4W	W	
	12	Junior World championships (heavy)	4F 4W	W	
1977	4	National championships Tokyo qualifier	7F 7W	W	
	4	Tokyo student championship +95kg	5F 5W	W	
	4	National championship	6F 6W	W	Youngest ever
	5	Tokyo student champions	3F 3W	TU won twice in a row	
	6	national student champions	5F 5W	TU W	
	7	National select categories + 95	4F 4W	W	
	10	Aomori National Youth championships	5F 5W	Kanagawa #2	
	10	National Students Kanto Kansai Tourna-ment	5F 4W 1D		
		" individuals	5F 4W 1L	#2	Lost to Yoshioka on a decision

*KG HS = Kyushu Gakuin High School
Up to October 1977 when he lost to Yoshioka at the National Students' Kansai-Kanto tournament, Yamashita had lost only 16 times. After that, from the Japan-USSR friendly onwards he did not lose a match. Practice fights; dan gradings and club visits are not included.
key: 10 – win by ippon (includes wins by injury and withdrawal)
       7 – win by waza-ari (or keikoku)
       5 – win by yuko (or chui)
       3 – win by koka (or shido)
       d – win by small margin e.g. decision   x – hikiwake (draw)

No	Yr./ mth	Competition	Opponent from		Score	Technique	Result
1	1977/10	Japan –USSR friendly	Guruuni	(USSR	10	yoko-shiho-gatame	
2	11	All Japan Select team Champions tournament	Eya	(Kanagawa)	10	kata-juiji-gatame	Tokai uni. #3
			Hosoya	(Kanagawa)	x		
			Kanui	(Kanagawa)	5	yuko: ko-soto-gake	
			Iwata	(Shin ni tetsu)	x		
3	11	Japan–USSR–France	Novikov	(USSR)	x		
			Novikov	(USSR)	x		
4	11	Tokyo students newcomers championships	Yoneyam	(Japan U)	10	osoto-gari	Tokai uni. #1
5			Furukawa	(Meiji U)	10	okuri-eri-jime	
6			Tsuchin	(Japan U)	10	ouchi-gari	
7	1978 2	Soviet Open over 95	Shirinian	(USSR)	10	uchimata	Won
8			Novikov	(USSR)	5	chui	
9			Gureefu	(USSR)	10	okuri-eri-jime	
10			Ojuarau	(Hungary)	10	okuri-eri-jime	
11			Nidzeradze	(USSR)	10	ouchi-uchimata	
12			Novikov	(USSR)	d	(decision)	
13			Nobakovski	(Poland)	10	yoko-shiho-gatame	
14			Gurin	(Poland)	10	tate-shiho-gatame	
15			Furamen	(GDR)	10	yoko-shiho-gatame	
16	2	Soviet Open Open category	Damadaev	(USSR)	10	uchimata	Won
17			Nidzeradze	(USSR)	10	yoko-shiho-gatame	
18			Turin	(USSR)	10	okuri-eri-jime	
19			Beliz	(USSR)	10	yoko-shiho-gatame	
20	4	All Japan Championships	Ito	(Ojisishi)	10	yoko-shiho-gatame	Won
21			Uemura	(Asahi Kasei)	d	(decision)	
22			Nakamura	(Tochigi police)	10	yoko-shiho-gatame	
23			Kawahara	(Aichi police)	10	yoko-shiho-gatame	
24			Takagi	(Keishicho)	10	osoto-gari	
25	5	Tokyo Students Championships	Kodakiri	(Keio U)	10	combination	Tokai U. 3rd win in a row.
26			?	(Komazawa U)	10	combination	
27			Hagiwara	(Nihon U)	10	uchimata	
28			Kanezawa	(Kokushikan)	10	combination	
29	6	National Students Championships	Sano	(Daikei Uni.)	10	uchimata	Tokai U. 2nd win in a row.
30			Yoshimota	(Kanezawako U)	10	uchimata	
31			Tasaka	((Daido U.)	10	yoko-shiho-gatame	
32			Ito	(Keisan U.)	10	yoko-shiho-gatame	
33			Kakuda	(Tenri U.)	10	yoko-shiho-gatame	
34	7	National select weight categories tournament	Matsui	(Tsukuba U.)	10	osoto-gari	
35			Yoshioka	(Chuo U.)	d	(decision)	
36			Uemura	(Asahi Kasei)	3	(koka – uchimata)	
37	9	Budokan Western Teams Invitation	Schneider	(FDR)	10		
38			Steib	(FDR)	10		
39			Kaban	(France)	10		
40			Van der Groeben	(FDR)	10		

41		Budokan Western Teams Invitation	Delban	(France)	10	yoko-shiho-gatame	
42			Parisi	(France)	10		
43			Fielli	(France)	x		
			Rouge	(France)	10		
44			Smetz	(Belgium)	*	overpowered	
45			Rouge	(France)	10	(unclear)	
46			Katsnekakov	(GDR)			
47		National Students Weight Category Tournament	Kimura	(Tenri U)	10	uchimata	
48			Kakuda	(Tenri U)	10	ouchi-gari	
49			Matsui	(Tsukuba)	10	okuri-eri-jime	Won
50			Yoshioka	(Chuo U)	10	ouchi-gari	
51		As above player's championship	Haraguchi	(Tokai U)	10	ochi-gari	2nd win in this champ-ionship in 2 years
52			Atsuta	(Meiji U)	10	yoko-shiho-gatame	
53			Kinoshita	(Kinki U)	10	uchimata	
54			Ito	(Keisan U)	10	ude-garami	
55			Endo	(Tokyo U)	10	yoko-shiho-gatame	
56		Nagano Cup (Youth)	Kawaguchi	(Toyama)	10	uchimata	Kana-gawa-Ken won
57	10		Yoshimura	(Tottori)	10	uchimata	
58			Tokunaga	(Osaka)	10	kaeshi-waza	
59			Watanabe	(Hyogo)	10	uchimata	
60			Endo	(Tokyo)	10	uchimata	
61		World University Championships	Noel	(France)	10	uchimata	Won
62			Elver	(FDR)	10	kuzure-kami-shiho	
63	11		Hindley	(GBR)	10	uchimata	
64			Smetz	(Belgium)	10	okuri-eri-jime	
65		Junior World Championships	Ives	(GBR)	10	uchimata	Won
66			Reszko	(Poland)	10	hiza-gatame	
67		World youth championships team competition	Unknown	(Belgium)	10	default	Japan #3
68	11		Unknown	(Netherlands)	10	okuri-eri-jime	
69			Nezugarashibiri	(USSR)	10	combination	
70			Unknown	(Brazil)	10	yoko-shiho-gatame	
		All Japan Select Teams Tournament	Iwata	(Shin Nitetsu)	x		Tokai U #3
71	11	Jigoro Kano International Tournament +95	Murier	(Brazil)	10	yoko-shiho-gatame	Won
72			Cho	(S.Korea)	10	uchimata YSG	
73			Rouge	(France)	10	yoko-shiho-gatame	
74			Uemura	(japan)	10	uchimata	
75		Jigoro Kano International Tournament Open	Turin	(USSR)	5	ouchi-gari	Won
76			Petroski	(Hungary)	10	uchimata	
77			Tripet	(France)	10	uchimata	
78			Iwata	(Japan)	10	yoko-shiho-gatame	
79			Rouge	(France)	5	osoto-gari	
80		French Open	Dobringe	(Austria)	10	ouchi-yoko-shiho	Won
81			Roberu	(France)	10	okuri-eri-jime	
82			Kotsan	(Czech)	10	osoto-kesa-gatame	
83			del Colombo	(France)	10	ouchi-gari	

84	1979	1	French Open	Nobokovski	(USSR)	10	uchimata	Won
85				Turin	(USSR)	10	yoko-shiho-gatame	
86		4	All Japan Championships	Masaki (Wagayama Kita)		10	osoto-gari	3rd win in a row
87				Muneta	(Ehine P)	10	yoko-shiho-gatame	
88				Yasukochi	(Kusan U)	10	yoko-shiho-gatame	
89				Matsui	(Meiji U)	10	kesa-gatame	
90				Endo	(keishicho)	10	uchi- KSG	
91		5	Tokyo Student's Championships	Takahashi	(KG U)	10	sukui-nage	Tokai U 4th win in a row
92				Yamamoto	(Tokyo U)	10	uchimata	
93				Kurihara	(Meiji U)	10	tate-shiho-gaatame	
94				Kaneko	(Nihon U)	10	ude-garami	
95		6	National Students champions' championship	Nagata	(Kyusan U)	10	kami-shiho-gatame	
96				Fujita	(Chuo U)	10	yoko-shiho-gatame	
97				Takano	(Tsukuba U)	10	yoko-shiho-gatame	
98				Mukoyama	(Kyosan U)	10	uchimata	
99				???????	(Nittai U)	10	ude-garami	
100		9	National select weight category championship	Matsui	(Tsukuba U)	7	ouchi	Won
101				Uemura	(Asahi Kasei)	d	(decision)	
102				Endo	(Keisicho)	10	uchimata-kesa	
103		10	National students weight category tournament	Ueguchi	(Kyusan U)	10	uchimata	
104				Hattori	(Doshisha)	10	kuzure-kami-shiho	
105				Hirama	(Tenri U)	10	kuzure-kami-shiho	
106				Kurihara	(Meiji U)	10	ouchi-gari	
107		10	As above players Championship	Kawabata	(Tokai U)	10	yoko-shiho-gatame	2 years in a row 3rd time win
108				Hanjo	(Kokushian)	10	okuri-eri-jime	
109				Yoneyama	(Nihon U)	10	yoko-shiho-gatame	
110				Hiram a	(Tenri U)	10	yoko-shiho-gatame	
111				Saito	(Kokushian)	10	kuzure-kami-shiho	
112		10	USA Open +95 category	Badger	(USA)	10	uchimata	Won
113				Thompson	(USA)	10	uchimata	
114		10	USA OPen OPen category	Anderson	(USA)	10	combination	Won
115				Bormark	(USA)	10	yoko-shiho-gatame	
116				Hirata	(Japan)	10	yoko-shiho-gatame	
117		12	World champion- ship +95 category	Gouok	(Indonesia)	10	uchimata	Won
118				Koroku	(Iran)	10	default	
119				Baruga	(Hungary)	10	kuzure-kami-shiho	
120				Turin	(USSR)	10	kuzure-kami-shiho	
121				Rouge	(France)	7	osoto-gari	
122	1980	1	National Select Team Competi- tion	Muneta	(Ehime P)	10	yoko--shiho-gatame	1st time Tokai U won
123				Iwata	(Shinnitetsu)	10	uchimata	
124				Takemaru	(Shinnitetsu)	10	uchimata-kesa	
125		2	Tokai U South Korean Tour	Chuu	(Korean JU)	10	okuri-eri-jime	4th win in a row
126				Chuu	(Korean JU)	10	osoto-gari	
127				?		10	uchimata	

206

128	4	All Japan Championships	Yamamoto	(Hokkaido P)	10	okuri-eri-jime	4th win in a row
129			Masaki	(Tsukuba)	10	yoko-shiho-gatame	
130			Takagi	(Keischo)	5	osoto	
131			Matsui	(Wagayama)	d	(decision)	
132			Endo	(Keischo)	10	yoko-shiho-gatame	
133	5	National select categories tournament +95	Matsui	(Tsukuba)	10	osoto-gari	4th win in a row
134			Takagi	(Keischo)	d	(decision)	
			Endo	(Keischo)	x	withdrew injured	
135	1981 4	All-Japan Championships	Ito	(Shiga p)	5	uchimata	5th win in a row
136			Kuramoto	(Kanagawa P)	10	uchimata	
137			Takagi	Police	10	uchimata YSG	
138			Matsui	(Tsukuba)	10	uchimata	
139			Endo	(Akita Keidai)	10	yoko-shiho-gatame	
140	9	World Championships +95 category	Gisrasson	(Iceland)	10	uchimata	2nd win in a row
141			Salonen	(Finland	10	uchimata	
142			Soler	(Spain)	10	yoko-shiho-gatame	
143			?	(S.Korea)	10	uchimata	
144			Verichev	(USSR)	10	yoko-shiho-gatame	
145		World Championships Open category	Mora	(Brasil)	10	yoko-shiho-gatame	Won
146			Berger	(Canada)	10	okuri-eri-jime	
147			Van de Walle	(Belgium)	10	uchimata	
148			Mitchell	(USA)	10	okuri-eri-jime	
149			Reszko	(Poland)	10	okuri-eri-jime	
150	10	Shiga Open Youth Section	Ogata	(Saga)	10	kesa-gatame	Kana-gawa Ken won
151			Naoyama	(Gifu)	10	uchimata-KG	
152			Hattori	(Kyoto)	10	yoko-shiho-gatame	
153			nakamura	(Ibaraki)	10	abandoned inj.	
154			Ishikawa	(Shizuoka)	10	osoto-KG	
155			Kubokama	(Shiga)	10	uchimata	
156	11	Japan Open +95	Kockman	(Czech)	10	okuri-ashi-harai	Won
157			Berger	(Canada)	5	chui	
158			Parisi	(France)	10	osoto-gari	
159			Metrishski	(USSR)	10	yoko-shiho-gatame	
160			Saito	(Kokushikan)	5	chui	
161	1982 4	All Japan Championships	Kawabata	(Aichi P)	10	combination	6th win in a row
162			Nakamura	(Nihon U)	10	osoto-guruma	
163			Nose	(Saitama)	10	okuri-eri-jime	
164			Hikage	(Iwate P)	10	yoko-shiho-gatame	
165			Matsui	(Tsukuba)	d	(decision)	
166	9	National Select Wt. Category Tournament +95	Fujihara	(Shinnitetsu)	10	yoko-shiho-gatame	5th win in 2 yrs.
167			Ito	(Shiga P)	5	uchimata	
168			Saito	(Kokushikan)	5	chui	
169	11	Jigoro Kano international Tournament Open caregory incl 95kg	?	(China)	10	Kosoto YSG	2nd win in a row
170			Turin	(USSR)	10	kuzure-kami-shiho	
171			Del Columbo	(France)	10	osoto-KG	
172			Masaki	(Tenri U)	10	osoto-gari	
173			Saito	(Kokushikan)	5	Ko-soto-gari	

174	11	Jigoro Kano	Salonen	(Finland)	10	okuri-eri-jime	Japan Won
175		international	Kokataylo	(GB)	10	yoko-shiho-gatame	
176		Tournament	Del Colombo	(France)	10	osoto-kesa-gatame	
177		Team competition	Turin	(USSR)	10	Default	
178	1983		Shiroda	(Fukkuoka)	10	yoko-shiho-gatame	7th win in a row
179	4	All Japan	Nakamura	(Tochigi)	10	ouchi-gari	
180		Championships	Suwa	(Keiyo Gasu)	10	okuri-eri-jime	
181			Fujihara	(Shin nitetsu)	10	osoto-gari	
182			Saito	(Kokushikan)	d	(decision)	
183	7	National Select	Fujihara	(Shin nitetsu)	10	osoto-gari	6th win in 2 years
184		Categorised	Masaki	(Tenri U)	10	kuzure-kami-shiho	
185		Tournament +95Kg	Saito	(Kokushikan)	3	(shido)	
186	10		Reszko	(Poland)	10	yoko-shiho-gatame	
187		World Champion-	Biktashev	(USSR)	10	okuri-eri-jime	
188		ships	Stoehr	(GDR)	3	(shido)	3rd win in a row
189		+95Kg	Willhelm	(Holland)	10	yoko-shiho-gatame	
190	1984	All Japan	Watanabe	(Akita)	10	kuzure-kami-shiho	
191	4	Championships	Takahashi	(Hokkaido P)	10	uchimata YSG	8th win in a row
192			Nakajima	(Saitama P)	10	uchimata	
193			Masaki	(Tenri U)	10	kuzure-kami-shiho	
194			Saito	(Kokushikan)	5	(Chui)	
195	8	Los Angeles	Coly	(Senegal)	10	ouchi-gaeshi	Won
196		Olympic Games	Schnabel	(FDR)	10	ouchi-gari	
197		Open Category	Del Columbo	(France)	10	ouchi-YSG	
198			Rashwan	(Egypt)	10	yoko-shiho-gatame	
199	1985	All Japan	Kuroda	(Yamagata P)	10	uchimata	
200	4	Championships	Osako	(Asahi kasei)	10	ouchi-gari	9th win in a row
201			Hikawa	(Tokai U)	10	yoko-shiho-gatame	
202			Masaki	(Tenri U)	10	yoko-shiho-gatame	
203			Saito	(Kokushikan)	d	(decision)	

KG   Kokugaku Gakuin Keisicho – Metropolitan Police Dojo
U – University   HS – High School P – Police

Out of a total of 559 competitions: 528 wins: 16 losses: 15 draws = 97.2 %
Techniques: out of the 203 consecutive wins recorded here, the techniques with which he scored his 164 wins are as follows:
(contests won due to abandonment not included.)
Yoko-shiho-gatame 45   Uchimata   35   Combination   23
Okuri-eri-jime   19   Kuzure-kami-shiho-gatame   11   Osoto-gari 9
Ouchi-gari 6   Ude-garami   3
Kami-shiho-gatame   2   Tate-shiho-gatame   2   Kesa-gatame   2
Kosoto-gari, Osoto-guruma,Ouchi-kaeshi, Kaeshi-waza, Kata-juji-gatame: 1 each

Opponents to whom losses occurred: Endo 4, Uemura 4, Yoshioka 2, Ninomiya 2 Matsui, Karui, Anzai, Takagi 1 each